PRENTICE HALL FOUNDATIONS OF PHILOSOPHY SERIES

D0162281

Virgil Aldrich	Philosophy of Art
William Alston	Philosophy of Language
David Braybrooke	Philosophy of Social Science
Roderick M. Chisholm	Theory of Knowledge, 3E
William Dray	Philosophy of History
C. Dyke	Philosophy of Economics
Joel Feinberg	Social Philosophy
Frederick Ferré	Philosophy of Technology
William K. Frankena	Ethics, 2E
Martin P. Golding	Philosophy of Law
Carl Hempel	Philosophy of Natural Science
John Hick	Philosophy of Religion, 3E
David L. Hull	Philosophy of Biological Science
Gerald C. MacCallum	Political Philosophy
D. L. C. Maclachlan	Philosophy of Perception
Joseph Margolis	Philosophy of Psychology
Wesley C. Salmon	Logic, 3E
Jerome Shaffer	Philosophy of Mind
Richard Taylor	Metaphysics, 3E

Elizabeth Beardsley and Tom L. Beauchamp, Editors
Monroe Beardsley, Founding Editor

Third Edition
THEORY OF KNOWLEDGE

Roderick M. Chisholm

Brown University

Prentice Hall, Englewood Cliffs, New Jersey 07632

LIBRARY OF CONGRESS
Library of Congress Cataloging-in-Publication Data

Chisholm, Roderick M.
    Theory of knowledge / by Roderick M. Chisholm. -- 3rd ed.
        p.   cm. -- (Prentice Hall foundations of philosophy series)
    Includes bibliographical references and index.
    ISBN 0-13-914177-4
    1. Knowledge, Theory of.   I. Title.   II. Series.
    BD161.C48 1989
    121--dc19   88-16882
                                                                 CIP

To My Wife

Manufacturing buyer: Peter Havens
Editorial/Production Supervision: Susan Alkana

 © 1989, 1977, 1966 by Prentice-Hall, Inc.
A Division of Simon & Schuster
Englewood Cliffs, New Jersey 07632

Printed in the United States of America

10 9 8 7 6 5 4 3 2 1

ISBN 0-13-914177-4

Prentice-Hall International (UK) Limited, *London*
Prentice-Hall of Australia Pty. Limited, *Sydney*
Prentice-Hall Canada Inc., *Toronto*
Prentice-Hall Hispanoamericana, S.A., *Mexico*
Prentice-Hall of India Private Limited, *New Delhi*
Prentice-Hall of Japan, Inc., *Tokyo*
Simon & Schuster Asia Pte. Ltd., *Singapore*
Editora Prentice-Hall do Brasil, Ltda., *Rio de Janeiro*

Contents

Foundations of Philosophy

Many of the problems of philosophy are of such broad relevance to human concerns, and so complex in their ramifications, that they are, in one form or another, perennially present. Though in the course of time they yield in part to philosophical inquiry, they may need to be rethought by each age in the light of its broader scientific knowledge and deepened ethical and religious experience. Better solutions are found by more refined and rigorous methods. Thus, one who approaches the study of philosophy in the hope of understanding the best of what it affords will look for both fundamental issues and contemporary achievements.

Written by a group of distinguished philosophers, the Foundations of Philosophy Series aims to exhibit some of the main problems in the various fields of philosophy as they stand at the present stage of philosophical history.

While certain fields are likely to be represented in most introductory courses in philosophy, college classes differ widely in emphasis, in method of instruction, and in rate of progress. Every instructor needs freedom to change his course as his own philosophical interests, the size and makeup of his class, and the needs of his students vary from year to year. The volumes in the Foundations of Philosophy Series—each complete in itself, but complementing the others—offer a new flexibility to the instructor, who can create his own textbook by combining several volumes as he wishes, and choose different combinations at different times. Those volumes that are not used in an introductory course will be found valuable, along with other texts or collections of readings, for the more specialized upper-level courses.

Elizabeth Beardsley / *Monroe Beardsley* / *Tom L. Beauchamp*

Preface

Since the publication in 1977 of the second edition of this book, there has been a resurgence of interest in the nature of knowledge. As a result, it is now possible to formulate the problems and proposed solutions with much greater precision than was possible ten years ago.

Contemporary interest in the nature of knowledge pertains not only to that branch of philosophy called "theory of knowledge" or "epistemology," but also to the fields of information theory, artificial intelligence, and cognitive science. The latter disciplines are not alternatives to the traditional theory of knowledge because they are branches of empirical science and not of philosophy. For the most part, the facts with which they are concerned are not relevant to the traditional philosophical questions. Unfortunately, however, this relevance has been exaggerated by many writers who do not seem to have grasped the traditional problems. I hope that the present book may help to correct this situation.

Much of the recent literature on the theory of knowledge has involved a criticism of "foundationalism" and "internalism," both terms being applicable to the general position set forth in the first two editions of this book. I believe that the most valuable function that can be performed by a third edition is to present, not a survey of all the conflicting views on the subject, but a defense of the traditional theory of knowledge from a "foundational" and "internal" point of view.

I wish to express my indebtedness to the many people with whom I have discussed these questions. These include: (1) the members of two seminars given at Brown in 1985 and 1986, the latter attended also by students from the University of Massachusetts in Amherst; (2) the members and participants of the Summer Seminar on Theory of Knowledge, sponsored by the Council for Philosophical Studies and given at the University of Colorado in Boulder in the summer of 1986; and (3) to the participants in the Colloquium on Epistemic Justification given at Brown University in November 1986.

I am especially indebted to Ernest Sosa, David Bennett, John Greco, and the publisher's reader who read and criticized early versions of this material.

I wish also to thank the editors and publishers of the following works for permission to reprint here certain portions of my writings: D. Reidel Publishing Company, Dordrecht, Holland, for excerpts from "An Analysis of Thirteen Epistemic Categories," from David F. Austin, ed., *Philosophical Analysis: A Defence by Example*," and for excerpts from "Epistemic Justification Internally Considered," from *Synthese*, Vol. 38 (1988); *Philosophical Perspectives*, Vol. II (1988), for excerpts from "The Evidence of the Senses."

CHAPTER 1

The Skeptic's Challenge

THE TRADITIONAL QUESTIONS

Theory of knowledge, when considered as a part of philosophy, is the concern with such questions as, "What can I know? How can I distinguish those things I am justified in believing from those things I am not justified in believing? And how can I decide whether I am more justified in believing one thing than in believing another?" These questions are properly called Socratic since they are questions about ourselves. Whatever the explanation for our interest in them may be (and providing causal explanations is no part of philosophy), the fact is that the epistemological questions do arise and that those for whom they arise take them very seriously. I propose that we try to take them seriously, too.

Our *purpose* in raising such questions is to correct and improve our own epistemic situation. Is it also that of attaining *knowledge*? It would be safer to say this: we want to do our best to improve our set of beliefs—to replace those that are unjustified by others that are justified and to replace those that have a lesser degree of justification with others that have a greater degree of justification.

THE PHILOSOPHICAL SKEPTIC

There are philosophers who doubt whether there is anything that we can know. They also doubt, therefore, whether it is possible for us to find out whether there is anything that we can know. Such philosophers—we may call them "philosophical skeptics"—may thus seem to present a challenge to traditional epistemology. Should we be deterred by this challenge?

The question is not whether we can *refute* philosophical skeptics. Nor is it even whether we can make them see that they are misguided. We are asking only whether they can provide us with reasons for thinking that we are misguided.

What can they tell us? There are several possibilities.

(I) They may say, "There are good reasons, after all, for supposing that we *cannot* know the kinds of things that most people think they can know." In support of this contention, one could provide an impressive amount of information about human fallibility. Suppose, then, we are given such information. Does the possession of such information mean that it is *not* reasonable for us to assume that we can answer our epistemological questions?

If we do have *information* about human fallibility, that is to say, if we *know* something about it, then, obviously, we should take such information into account when we ask about what it is that we can know. But we should *also* take into account the fact that, despite the indications of fallibility, whatever these indications may be, we *are* aware of them and therefore *do* have information about ourselves and other people.

(II) The skeptics may tell us various things about human fallibility but without professing to be justified in thinking that these things are really true. What should we say to them in *this* case? We may say, tautologically, that we have ground for doubting only if we have *ground* for doubting. But how could something we are *not* justified in believing provide us with a ground for skepticism?

(III) There are the contentions of what we may call the "perhaps-you-are-wrong" skeptics. They will point out to us that Descartes' supposition of a malicious demon is logically possible. And it is true that no *contradiction* is involved in assuming that all my present experiences are caused by such an evil spirit. Therefore, skeptics conclude, it is not reasonable for me to have the beliefs that I do about the things around me.

A contemporary version of this reasoning has been suggested by Hilary Putnam:

Imagine that a human being (you can imagine this to be yourself) has been subjected to an operation by an evil scientist. The person's brain (your brain) has been removed from the body and placed in a vat of nutrients which keeps the brain alive. The nerve endings have been connected to a super-scientific computer which causes the person whose brain it is to have the illusion that everything is perfectly normal. There seem to be people, objects, the sky, etc; but really all the person (you) is experiencing is the result of electronic impulses traveling from the computer to the nerve endings.[1]

---

[1] Hilary Putnam, *Reason, Truth and History* (Cambridge, England: Cambridge University Press, 1981), pp. 5–6.

The type of skeptics we are now envisaging will say to us, "It is logically possible that you are now in such a predicament. Therefore you are not justified in believing, as you do, that you exist outside the vat of nutrients." These skeptics are not saying, of course, that we are justified in believing that we *are* in the vat. They are saying that we are *not* justified in believing that we are *not* in the vat.

Is this a good argument? Its structure is something like this:

(1)   You now have certain experiences which you believe result from your present perceptions of the things around you and from the memories you have had of other such perceptions.

(2)   It is logically possible that (i) you have experiences of the kind that you now have and (ii) that these experiences are brought about, not by the perception of physical things around you, but by a malicious demon who is doing strange things to your brain.

Therefore

(3)   You are not justified in believing that you are now surrounded by familiar physical things and human beings.

What are we to say of this argument?

The reply is very simple: the conclusion does not follow from the premises. It takes no great logical acumen to see that no logical contradiction is involved in affirming the premises and at the same time denying the conclusion.[2]

What, then, is the move of the skeptics? The only possibility is for them to introduce a *third* premise—one which will be such that the conjunction of it with (1) and (2) does yield the conclusion (3). But what would this third premise be? And how would the skeptics defend it?

They would need to add a premise of this sort:

> If those of your experiences which you think are perceptions and memories are such that it is logically possible to have those experiences without perceiving or remembering anything, then you are not justified in believing that you are now perceiving external things or remembering past events.

At this point we should be sophisticated enough to challenge the skeptic's premise, "And what is *your* ground for affirming that? What justification do you have for thinking that your complex philosophical proposition is more reasonable for me than the belief that I am surrounded by familiar physical things?"

---

[2] Compare G. E. Moore's essay, "Four Forms of Scepticism," in his *Philosophical Papers* (London: George Allen and Unwin, 1959), pp. 196–225; Compare Peter Klein, *A Refutation of Skepticism* (Minneapolis, MN: University of Minnesota Press, 1981); and Barry Stroud, *The Philosophical Significance of Skepticism* (Oxford: Oxford University Press, 1984)

It is not easy to think of any plausible reply that the skeptics might make.

Perhaps the hope of the skeptics is to produce a kind of *reductio ad absurdum* argument, proving to us that, if we do act upon the presuppositions we have cited, then we will find that, after all, we do not have any justified beliefs. Perhaps the skeptics hope for this: after we have done our work and have set forth a theory of knowledge, then they can do *their* work and show that what we think we know justifies us in believing that we cannot know those things. But since they have not yet done this work, the mere possibility that they will does not provide us with any positive ground for skepticism.

What we have been saying, of course, is not likely to convince the skeptics and we can hardly claim to have "refuted" them. But our question was not, "Can we refute the skeptics?" Our question was: "Are there positive reasons for being skeptical about the possibility of succeeding in the epistemic enterprise?" The answer seems to be that there are no such reasons. And therefore it is not unreasonable for us to continue.

EPISTEMOLOGISTS' FAITH IN THEMSELVES

Consider just one of the traditional questions:

(A)   What am I justified in believing?

Once we ask this question, a second question forces itself upon us—a question about the first question:

(B)   What am I justified in presupposing when I try to find out what I am justified in believing?

If I'm not justified in making *any* presuppositions when I try to answer the first question, then I will have no reasonable way of evaluating any of the answers that may come to mind. Indeed, if I'm not justified in making any presuppositions, I will not be justified in affirming the statement that I have just made—or in affirming the present statement. What kind of presupposition, then, *could* I be justified in making? Certain things are presupposed by the fact that one is able to *ask* the questions.

The ability to ask, "What can I know?" and "What am I justified in believing?" presupposes that one has the concepts of knowledge and of epistemic justification. If I can ask what it is that I know or can know and if I can ask whether I am more justified in believing some things than in believing other things, then I have some understanding of *what it is* to know something and of *what it is* to be justified or to be unjustified in believing something. "It would be absurd to look for something if one had no idea at all of what one is looking for.[3] This means that I am capable of at least figuring out what it *would* be to have an epistemically respectable set of beliefs.

One type of presupposition, then, may be summarized as follows:

(P1)   I have an idea of what it is for a belief to be justified and I have an idea of what it is for a belief not to be justified; I have an idea of what it is to *know* something; and I have an idea of what it is for one thing to be *more justified* for me than another.

Instead of saying, "I have an idea of what it is for a belief to be justified," one may say "I can *conceive* what it is for a belief to be justified." (A person may have a concept, of course, without being able to define or analyse the content of that concept. But if one has a given concept, then one may be able to assess the adequacy of a proposed definition or analysis of that concept.)

In trying to answer these questions, I consider my various beliefs and try to order or rank them with respect to their justification. This presupposes that I can know something about my beliefs and present state of mind. I would say, then, that the traditional epistemologist is justified in making the following presupposition:

(P2)   I am justified in believing that I can improve and correct my system of beliefs. Of those beliefs that are about matters of interest or concern to me, I can eliminate the ones that are unjustified and add others that are justified, and I can replace less justified beliefs about those topics by beliefs about them that are more justified.

If this presupposition is true, then there are some properties such that, if I have them, then I can be said to know directly that I have them.

This second presupposition provides a reason for calling traditional epistemology "internalistic." One presupposes that there are certain things one can know about oneself without the need of any outside assistance.

In making their assumptions, epistemologists presuppose that they are *rational* beings. This means, in part, that they have certain properties which are such that, if they ask themselves, with respect to any one of these properties, whether or not they have that property, then it will be evident to them that they have it. It means further that they are able to know what they think and believe and that they can recognize inconsistencies.

Epistemologists presuppose, then, that they can succeed. This means, therefore, that they have a kind of faith in themselves.[4]

---

[3] Bernard Bolzano, *Was ist Philosophie?* (Vienna: Wilhelm Braumüller, 1849), p. 7.

[4] "The only security we have in the quest for truth is our trust in our own intellectual powers to reach our objective and the sense not to fall into needless error." Keith Lehrer, "Self-Profile," in R. J. Bogdan, ed., *Profiles: Keith Lehrer* (Dordrecht: D. Reidel, 1981), p. 98.

ON THE JUSTIFICATION OF THIS FAITH

Am I justified in making such presuppositions?

There are three possible belief-attitudes that I may take with respect to the proposition that this faith in myself *is* justified: (1) I may *deny* the proposition; or (2) I may *affirm* the proposition; or (3) I may *withhold* the proposition. If I *deny* that the faith is justified, then it would hardly be reasonable for me to pursue the task of traditional epistemology. And if I *affirm* that the faith is justified, then I will be faced with questions about justification once again—this time questions about my justification for believing that the traditional presuppositions are justified. The wise epistemologist, therefore, would provisionally *withhold* belief in the proposition that his faith is justified.

One may object, "But it is unreasonable to proceed if you do not think you are justified in proceeding!" The answer is, of course, that *that* is not unreasonable. What *is* unreasonable is to procede when you think you are *not* justified in proceeding. And from the fact that you do *not* think you *are* justified, it does not follow that you do think you are not justified.

THE PROBLEM OF THE CRITERION

We cannot, however, escape the challenge of the ancient "problem of the criterion." The problem may be put briefly as follows.

We may distinguish two very general questions. These are "*What* do we know?" and "How are we to decide, in any particular case, *whether* we know?" The first of these may also be put by asking, "What is the *extent* of our knowledge?" and the second by asking, "What are the *criteria* of knowing?"

If we know the answer to either one of these questions, then, perhaps, we may devise a procedure that will enable us to answer the other. If we can specify the criteria of knowledge, we may have a way of deciding how far our knowledge extends. Or if we know how far our knowledge does extend and are able to say what the things are that we know, then we may be able to formulate criteria enabling us to mark off the things we do know from those that we do not.

But if we do not have the answer to the first question, then, it would seem, we have no way of answering the second. And if we do not have the answer to the second, then, it would seem, we have no way of answering the first.

Is there a way out? There are two possibilities.

(1) We may try to find out what we know or what we are justified in believing without making use of any *criterion* of knowledge or of justified belief. Or (2) we may try to formulate a criterion of knowledge without

appeal to any *instances* of knowledge or of justified belief. In the first case, we would be "particularists" and in the second "generalists" or "methodists."

I have assumed that we can know something about our beliefs. I can know, for example, that I believe that there are dogs. But in order to find out that I believe that there are dogs, I did not need to apply any criterion stating *how* one can know that one believes that there are dogs.

And so, it would seem, we begin as "particularists": we identify *instances* of knowing without applying any *criteria* of knowing or of justification.[5]

Given what we have presupposed, we may say, in the words of D. J. Mercier, that the concept of epistemic justification is *objective, internal,* and *immediate*.[6] It is *internal* and *immediate* in that one can find out directly, by *reflection*, what one is justified in believing at any time. And epistemic justification is *objective* in that it can itself constitute an object of justification and knowledge. It is possible to know that we know and it is possible to be justified in believing.

Now, I think, we may characterize the concept of "internal justification" more precisely. If a person S is *internally justified* in believing a certain thing, then this may be something he can know just by reflecting upon his own state of mind. And if S is thus internally justified in believing a certain thing, can he also know, just by reflecting upon his state of mind, that he *is* justified in believing that thing? This, too, is possible—once he has acquired the concept of epistemic justification.

Let us now consider the concept of epistemic justification in more detail.

---

[5] "The Academicians claim that had truth no hallmark, to discover truth would be as difficult as to identify a fugitive if we know none of his distinguishing features. But this is ridiculous. Light, to be distinguished from darkness, needs no special mark; so the truth needs no mark save the enveloping clarity that surrounds it and persuades the mind despite its objections." A. Arnauld, *The Art of Thinking* (1683) (Indianapolis, IN: The Bobbs-Merrill Co., 1964), p. 11.

[6] D. J. Mercier, *Critériologie Générale ou Théorie Générale de la Certitude*, Eighth Edition (Louvain: Institut Supérieur de Philosophie, 1923), p. 234. Mercier applied these terms to what he called "criteria" or "marks of truth." The first edition of his work appeared in 1899.

CHAPTER 2

Epistemic Justification

EPISTEMIC JUSTIFICATION

The term "justify," in its application to a belief, is a term of epistemic appraisal: it is used to say something about the reasonableness of that belief. So, too, are such terms as "evident," "gratuitous," "certain," and "probable." And "reasonable" itself may be a term of epistemic appraisal.

Most epistemic concepts presuppose a single relational concept that may be expressed by saying, "So-and-so is *at least as justified* for S as is such-and-such." The expressions "so-and-so" and "such-and-such" may be replaced by terms denoting "believings" and "withholdings." (A person may be said to *withhold* a proposition h provided he does not believe h and does not believe the negation of h. The proposition that God exists is such that the theist accepts it, the atheist accepts its negation, and the agnostic withholds it.)

"More justified," of course, may be explicated by reference to "at least as justified." For to say that A is *more* justified for S than B is to say that it is false that B is *at least* as justified for S as is A.

Here are two clearcut examples of this use of "more justified than."

(1) St. Augustine suggests that, even though there may be ground to question the reliability of the senses, most of us are *more justified* most of the time in believing that we *can* rely upon them than in believing that we can *not* rely upon them.[1]

---

[1] This thesis is suggested by St. Augustine in his polemics against the skeptics. Compare his *Against the Academicians* (Milwaukee, WI: Marquette University Press, 1942). The thesis is

(2) Even if there happens to be life on Venus, most of us are more justified in withholding belief about the presence of life there than we are in believing that life exists there.

We have been speaking about what a *person*, or subject, is justified in believing. We may say, for example, that the person S is at least as justified in believing p as he is in withholding p. Such statements about the person entitle us to say something about the epistemic status of the relevant proposition *for* that person. For example, if S is at least as justified in believing p as he is in withholding p, then the proposition p is *beyond reasonable doubt* for S. Being beyond reasonable doubt, then, is one of many epistemic categories into which a propositon p may fall.

We now consider these categories in more detail.

THE COUNTERBALANCED

If a proposition is *counterbalanced* for a given subject, then neither the proposition nor its negation has any positive degree of epistemic justification for that subject.

D1   p is counterbalanced for S = Df   S is at least as justified in believing p as in believing the negation of p; and S is at least as justified in believing the negation of p as in believing p

The Greek skeptic, Pyrrho of Elis (c. 365–275 B.C.), seems to have held that all propositions are counterbalanced. Some of the later Greek skeptics (the "Academics") expressed this doctrine by saying that all propositions can be *shown* to be counterbalanced. But this would be contradictory.[2] The assumption that we *are* justified in supposing that every proposition is counterbalanced, presupposes that *that* proposition, at least, is *not* counterbalanced.

The term *"Pyrrhonism"* is sometimes used to refer to the following doctrine: trying to avoid having *unjustified* belief is more reasonable than trying to *have* justified belief. Pyrrhonism, as we will see, is not presupposed by the present book.

---

explicitly formulated by Bertrand Russell in *An Inquiry into Meaning and Truth* (New York: W. W. Norton & Company, Inc., 1940), p. 166: "Beliefs caused by perception are to be accepted unless there are positive grounds for rejecting them."

[2] "Montaigne writes that the Academicians differ from the Pyrrhonists in maintaining that some things are more probable than others, a position the Pyrrhonists will not allow. Then he goes on to side with the Pyrrhonists, saying 'The doctrine of the Pyrrhonists is bolder and much more likely.' So there are some things more likely than others!" Antoine Arnauld, *The Art of Thinking* (Indianapolis, IN.: The Bobbs-Merrill Company, Inc., 1964), p. 10. This work was first published in 1662 as *La Logique, ou l'Art de Penser*.

THE PROBABLE

If a proposition is not counterbalanced for S, then either that proposition or its negation is *probable* for S. We here take the term "probable" in that sense in which all of us understand it—whether or not we know anything about epistemology, statistics, or inductive logic. That is the sense we may have in mind when we ask ourselves such questions as, "Is it probable that I will be alive a year from now?" and "Is it probable that it will rain tomorrow?"

To say that a proposition is probable for us, in this fundamental sense, is to say simply that we are more justified in believing that proposition than in believing its negation. Our definition, then, is this:

D2   p is probable for S = Df   S is more justified in believing p than in
                believing the negation of p

If it is probable for you, in this sense, that you will be alive a year from now, then you are more justified in believing you will be alive a year from now than in believing you will not be alive a year from now. This fundamental sense of "probability" has been the concern of epistemologists since at least the time of the Greek skeptics.[3]

Propositions which are thus probable for a person S and which are *merely probable* for S (they have no higher epistemic status for S), may yet be such that some are *more justified* for S than are others. It is, at best, only probable for you that you will be alive a year from now; and it is, at best, only probable for you that you will be alive six months from now. But you are *more justified* in believing that you will be alive six months from now than in believing that you will be alive a year from now. In this case, we may say, of two propositions each of which is merely probable for you, that one of them is *more probable* for you than the other.

We must take care to distinguish this fundamental epistemic sense of "probable" from the sense that that expression has in statistics and in inductive logic. In those disciplines "probable" is defined in terms of frequency of occurrence—sometimes in terms of "the limit of relative frequency in the long run." But the epistemic concept of probability, although it is closely connected with the concept of frequency, is a concept of a very different sort. (We consider this topic in more detail in Chapter 6).

THAT WHICH IS BEYOND REASONABLE DOUBT

We have already said what it is for a proposition to be beyond reasonable doubt:

[3] See Cicero, *De Natura Deorum, Academica*, Loeb Classical Library (New York: G. P. Putnam's Sons, 1933); e.g., *De Academica*, Vol. II, xxxix (pp. 588, 600. Cicero uses *"probabilitas."*

D3   p is beyond reasonable doubt for S = Df   S is more justified in believing p than in withholding p

The category of being *beyond reasonable doubt* is illustrated by the proposition that the building in which I now find myself will be here tomorrow. The proposition is not evident. But for me—and I hope that for others—the proposition is such that believing it is more justified than withholding it.

Obviously there are some *true* propositions which are such that we are more justified in believing them than in withholding them. Are there also *false* propositions which we are more justified in believing than in withholding? We will find that this may well be true. Or, more exactly, we will find that, if philosophical skepticism is false, and if, as a matter of fact, we do know many of the things about the world that we now think we know, then it is quite possible that some false propositions are such that it is more reasonable for us to believe those propositions than it is for us to withhold them.

THE EVIDENT

The evident is that which, when added to true belief, yields knowledge.

There are, presumably, nine planets. The person who *believes* that there are nine planets but does not *know* that there are has at least true belief about the number of planets. But a person who knows that there are nine planets has something that the person who has mere true belief does not have. The traditional way of putting this difference is to say that, for the person who has knowledge, the true proposition believed is also *evident*.

One should not confuse the locution "p is evident for S" with "S has adequate evidence for p." The latter expression, but not the former, may be taken to mean, "Those things that are evident for S make p beyond reasonable doubt for S."

An evident proposition, like one that is beyond reasonable doubt, is a proposition which is such that one has more justification for believing it than for withholding it. And the evident has this further feature: for any two propositions, if one of them is evident, then believing the one that is evident is at least as justified as *withholding the other*—whatever epistemic status the other may have. And so the evident may be characterized this way:

D4   p is evident for S = Df   For every proposition q, believing p is at least as justified for S as is withholding q

If it is now evident to you that the sun is shining, then, given this definition, we may say that you are at least as justified in believing that the sun is shining as you are in withholding any contradiction or in withholding what is epistemically impossible (say, the proposition you would express by saying "I am not thinking"). This conception of the evident reflects the rejection of Pyrrhonism.

We have noted that a proposition may be beyond reasonable doubt and also false. We will find that the same is true of the evident. It is possible that there are some propositions which are both *evident* and false.[4] This fact makes the theory of knowledge more difficult than it otherwise would be and it has led some philosophers to wonder whether, after all, the things we know might not be restricted to those things that are absolutely certain. But if we do in fact know some of those ordinary things that we think we know (for example, that there are such and such pieces of furniture in the room, that the sun was shining yesterday, that the earth has existed for many years past) then we must reconcile ourselves to the possibility that on occasion some of those things that are evident to us are also false.

THE CERTAIN

Epistemic certainty may be characterized this way:

D5   p is certain for S = Df   For every q, believing p is more justified for S than withholding q, and believing p is at least as justified for S as is believing q

This concept is illustrated by those propositions about mental life that are sometimes called "self-presenting." It is also illustrated by certain logical and metaphysical axioms that form the basis of what we know *a priori*. We will discuss these types of certainty in the following two chapters.

FORMAL EPISTEMIC PRINCIPLES

We have taken "at least as justified as" as an undefined locution. Obviously, we have to take *some* locution as undefined. But the fact that we have not defined it does not mean that we cannot say anything about what is intended by it. If we set forth certain axioms for the locution, we can illuminate just what it is that we intend to express by it.

Let us note, then, some of the basic principles governing the use of "at least as justified as." We first formulate two very general principles, telling us that the justification relation is asymmetrical and transitive:

(A1)   If A is more justified than B for S, then B is not more justified than A for S

---

[4] Pierre Bayle may have been the first to have called attention to this fact. See his *Historical and Critical Dictionary: Selections*, ed. Richard H. Popkin (Indianapolis, IN: Bobbs-Merrill Company, Inc., 1965), pp. 199–201.

(A2)   If A is more justified than B for S, and if B is more justified than C for S, then A is more justified than C for S

Other principles will tell us more about the strictly *epistemic* content of "at least as justified as" and will throw light on some of the most fundamental questions of the theory of knowledge. I will list three such principles. The first two are anti-Pyrrhonian and the third may be called the *objectivity* principle. Commitment to these principles is essential to the view set forth in this book.

TWO ANTI-PYRRHONIAN PRINCIPLES

William James wrote:

> There are two ways of looking at our duty in the matter of opinion—ways entirely different, and yet ways about whose difference the theory of knowledge seems hitherto to have shown little concern. We *must know* the truth; and we *must avoid error*—these are our first and great commandments as would-be knowers; but they are not two ways of stating an identical commandment, they are two separable laws.[5]

One fundamental issue may be put by asking: Which of these two "commandments" should be given the greater weight? Or, more generally, is it more reasonable to try to reach the truth or to try to avoid error?

It is sometimes said that playing it safe is always more reasonable than taking any chances. And this would seem to be the attitude of the Pyrrhonist with respect to what it is reasonable for us to believe. But the following principle is "anti-Pyrrhonian":

(A3)   If the conjunction p&q is beyond reasonable doubt for S, then believing p&q is more justified for S than believing p while withholding q

This principle describes conditions under which one is more justified in believing *more* rather than in believing *less*. In other words, it tells us that "playing it safe" is not always the most reasonable course.

Given this common sense principle, we may say that, if believing p is more justified than withholding p and if believing q is more justified than withholding q, then believing the conjunction of the *two* propositions, p and q, is more justified than believing just *one* of the two conjuncts and withholding the other. If "John is a musician" is beyond reasonable doubt and if "John's brother is a musician" is also beyond reasonable doubt, then accepting the conjunction, "John is a musician and John's brother is a musician," is more justified than accepting just one of the two conjuncts.

---

[5] William James, *The Will to Believe and Other Essays in Popular Philosophy* (New York: David McKay Co., Inc., 1911), p. 17.

The principle also applies in a significant way to propositions we would not ordinarily express as conjunctions. Suppose that "I see a person" and "I see a person sitting" are both justified for me. In this case, "I see a person" is *safer* than "I see a person sitting." But our principle tells us that, of two propositions both of which are beyond reasonable doubt for S and one of which is richer in content but less safe than the other, accepting the safer proposition while withholding the one that is richer in content may be *less* justified for S than accepting the one that is richer in content.

Our second "anti-Pyrrhonian" principle is this:

(A4)   If anything is probable for S, then something is certain for S

As we will see, this type of principle is one feature of what is called "foundationalism" in the theory of knowledge. Many philosophers attempt to dispense with it. We will discuss its implications in Chapters 3 and 9.

THE OBJECTIVITY PRINCIPLE

We turn now to what may be called the *objectivity* principle. This principle pertains to the fact that we can sometimes know that we know. If knowledge is justified true belief and if we ever know that we know, then we sometimes know that we are justified in believing. And if we can ever know that we are justified in believing, then epistemic statements—say, "It is evident for S that the sun is shining"—are (1) statements that are either *true* or *false* and (2) statements that can be *known* to be true or *known* to be false. It follows that epistemic statements are, in D. J. Mercier's terms, *objective*: they are not mere expressions of confidence or of other feelings.[6] A further consequence would be that if epistemic statements are to be construed as *normative* statements, then, contrary to one widespread philosophical belief, some normative statements express what is true or what is false and are capable of being known to be true or known to be false.

Under what conditions, then, *could* we obtain knowledge about epistemic justification? Bertrand Russell once wrote: "The degree of credibility attaching to a proposition is itself sometimes a datum. I think we should also hold that the degree of credibility to be attached to a *datum* is sometimes a datum, and sometimes (perhaps always) falls short of certainty."[7]

---

[6] *Critériologie Générale ou Théorie Générale de la Certitude*, Eighth Edition (Louvain: Institut Supérieur de Philosophy), p. 234. For a general discussion of this point of view, compare Noah M. Lemos, "Two Types of Epistemic Evaluative Cognitivism," *Philosophical Studies*, Vol. 49 (1986), pp. 313–328.

[7] Bertrand Russell, *Human Knowledge: Its Scope and Limits* (New York: Simon & Schuster, 1948), p. 381. Russell's expression "degree of credibility" may suggest our "level of justification," but he uses the expression more narrowly and, indeed, may be said to define it in terms of (i) the probability or confirmation relation and (ii) the evident. He writes: "When in relation to all the available evidence, a proposition has a certain mathematical probability, then this measures its degree of credibility" (p. 381).

But in what sense is epistemic justification a datum? Certainly we do not experience a *quality* that might be called the evidence of a proposition.

The *objectivity* principle tells us what *kind* of justification we can have for beliefs *about* justification:

(A5)   If S knows that p, then, if S believes that he knows that p, then S knows that he knows that p

What could we say to one who does not believe that this principle is true? We could cite the following preanalytic data: (i) people often know that they know (I know that I know that I'm in Rhode Island); and (ii) people know such things without having any specialized information about epistemology or the theory of epistemic justification. Hence (iii) when we know that p, it may be the case, not only that there is an experience that makes it known to us that p, but also that there is an experience that can make it known to us that we *know* that p. But what would the second experience be? Our objectivity principle tells us, in effect, that the second experience is the same as the first. What else, after all, *is* there to make it known to us that we know that p?[8]

We will return to "knowing that one knows" in Chapter 10.

THE 13 STEPS

We note, finally, that our undefined epistemic concept and the axioms that may be provided for it enable us to set forth a hierarchy of epistemic concepts. This hierarchy involves 13 epistemic categories—13 steps or stages each capable of being occupied by countless propositions.

To see the point of such a hierarchy, let us turn back to the concept of *the evident*. An evident proposition is one that is justified. But there are many justified propositions that are not evident. Indeed many propositions that may be said to have a *very high degree* of justification are not evident. For example, it may be evident to you now that you have walked today and that you also walked yesterday and the day before that. You may have very good grounds for accepting the proposition that you will walk tomorrow and the day after that: the proposition may be strongly supported by induction.[9] But it is not now *evident* to you or to anyone else that you will walk tomorrow. For no one now *knows* that you will walk tomorrow.

The proposition that you will walk tomorrow may be *beyond reasonable doubt* for you. But nothing that you can find out *today* can make it *evident* for you today that you will walk tomorrow.

---

[8] Since our formulation of this principle contains the word "know," we have gone beyond the concepts that we have defined in terms of "at least as justified as." In the final chapter, however, "know" will be defined in terms of these concepts.

[9] The concept of inductive support will be discussed in Chapter 6.

The difference between what is evident and what is beyond reasonable doubt but not evident is not a mere *quantitative* difference. It is a *qualitative* difference, like that between being in motion and being at rest. It is also comparable to the distinction between the situation wherein one is conscious and has auditory sensations and that wherein one is conscious and has no auditory sensations. And it is comparable to the distinction between the situation wherein one is alive and conscious and that wherein one is alive but not conscious.

Propositions that are *counterbalanced* may be thought of as occupying the zero-level. Those that are *probable* may be thought of as occupying the lowest positive epistemic level. Above these are propositions that are *beyond reasonable doubt*. Still higher are propositions that are *evident*. And at the top of the hierarchy are those propositions that are *certain*.

There are two additional positive steps or levels that we have not mentioned. One is the step between that which is probable and that which is beyond reasonable doubt. Propositions in this category may be *epistemically in the clear*." A proposition is said to be epistemically in the clear for a subject S provided only that S is *not* more justified in withholding that proposition than in believing it. The other positive step falls between the evident and the certain; propositions in this category are said to be "*obvious*." A proposition p is said to be obvious for a subject S provided only that, for every proposition q, S is more justified in believing p than in withholding q.

So far, we have one zero level and six positive levels. We may now go on to distinguish six *negative* levels. The negative level that a proposition occupies is a function of the positive level of its negation. Thus the "highest" negative level that a proposition p may occupy for a subject S is that of being such that its negation is probable for S. And the "lowest" negative level is that of having a negation that is certain for S.

Our epistemic hierarchy, then, may be put this way:

  6. Certain
  5. Obvious
  4. Evident
  3. Beyond Reasonable Doubt
  2. Epistemically in the Clear
  1. Probable
  0. Counterbalanced
 -1. Probably False
 -2. In the Clear to Disbelieve
 -3. Reasonable to Disbelieve
 -4. Evidently False
 -5. Obviously False
 -6. Certainly False

The first five categories are such that each includes but is not included in the category listed immediately below it. And the last five categories are

such that each includes but is not included in the category listed immediately above it.[10]

To see the point of such a hierarchy, let us turn back to the concept of *the
evident*. An evident proposition is one that is justified. But there are many
justified propositions that are not evident. Indeed many propositions that
may be said to have a *very high degree* of justification are not evident. For
example, it may be evident to you now that you have walked today and that
you also walked yesterday and the day before that. You may have very
good grounds for accepting the proposition that you will walk tomorrow
and the day after that: the proposition may be strongly supported by
induction.[11] But it is not now *evident* to you or to anyone else that you will
walk tomorrow, for no one now *knows* that you will walk tomorrow.

The proposition that you will walk tomorrow may be *beyond reasonable
doubt* for you, but nothing that you can find out *today* can make it *evident* for
you today that you will walk tomorrow.

---

[10] A further principle that is needed to complete our hierarchy of 13 steps may be summarized this way: If a proposition p epistemically in the clear for S, then p is probable for S.
Instances of it are: "If agnosticism is not more justified for S than theism, then theism is more
justified for S than atheism"; and "If agnosticism is not more justified for S than atheism, then
atheism is more justified for S than theism." The point of including this principle here is to
insure that whatever is epistemically in the clear is also probable.

[11] The concept of inductive support will be discussed in Chapter 6.

Certainty and the Self-Presenting

SELF-PRESENTATION

It has been said that our sensations present us with things *other* than themselves and that, in so doing, they also present *themselves*. The thought is this: if, for example, you look outside and see a dog, then you see it by means of visual sensations that are called up as a result of the way the dog is related to your eyes and nervous system. In seeing the dog, you are also aware of the visual sensations (but it would be a mistake to say that you *see* them). Whether sensations ever *do* present us with such things as dogs is a difficult question which we will discuss in Chapter 5. We will now consider the simpler question: whether sensations and certain other properties may be said to present us with *themselves*.[1]

There is a clear sense in which sensations *do* present themselves to us. And so, too, for such properties as dreaming, imagining, hoping, wondering, fearing, liking, and disliking.

In order to put more clearly what is being said, we will formulate a *definition* of "self-presenting property" and then we will formulate a general *principle* about the epistemic status of such properties.

---

[1]This view of sensations is suggested by A. Meinong, *On Emotional Presentation*, edited and translated by M. S. Kalsi (Evanston, Il: Northwestern University Press, 1972), Sec. 1. Compare also Franz Brentano, *Psychology from an Empirical Standpoint* (London: Routledge & Kegan Paul, 1972), Chap. 2. Sec. 2; C. J. Ducasse, "Propositions, Truth, and the Ultimate Criterion of Truth," in *Philosophy and Phenomenological Research*, Vol. IV (1944), pp. 317–340; Roderick Firth, "The Anatomy of Certainty," *The Philosophical Review*, Vol. 76 (1967), pp. 3–27; and William J. Alston, "Varieties of Privileged Access," *American Philosophical Quarterly*, Vol. 8 (1971), pp. 223–241.

A self-presenting property is of this sort: from the fact that you have it, it follows logically that you are *thinking*, but it does *not* follow logically that you have any properties that do not include thinking. (Of course, it is physically or causally necessary that, in order to think, you must have a brain and therefore many physiological properties. But it is not *logically* necessary that if you think then you have such properties.)

Our definition is this:

> P is self-presenting = Df   Every property that P entails includes the property of thinking

The words "include" and "entail," as they are to be taken here, call for comment.

One property may be said to *include* another if the first is necessarily such that anything that has it also has the second. And the property of being F may be said to *entail* the property of being G provided that believing something to be F includes believing something to be G.[2]

The property of *riding* a bicycle, unlike the property of *thinking about* riding a bicycle, entails a property it does not include—namely, the property of being a bicycle. One doesn't need to *be* a bicycle in order to think about riding a bicycle.

Such self-presenting properties are a source of certainty. If you think about riding a bicycle, then you have all the justification you need for *believing* that you are thinking about riding a bicycle. The example illustrates a more general principle:

M1   If the property of being F is self-presenting, if S is F, and if S believes himself to be F, then it is certain for S that he is F

Self-presenting properties, then, are a source of certainty. But we should remind ourselves of what we have said about certainty. In saying that it is "certain" for a person S that he is F, we are *not* saying that S *feels certain* that he is F. In the case of most self-presenting properties, one may have no feeling at all about the question whether or not one has them. We are using "certain" to refer to the epistemic category we distinguished in the previous chapter. We are saying, for example, that if feeling sad is a self-presenting property and if S feels sad, then S is at least as justified in believing that he feels sad as he is in having any other belief.

Some self-presenting properties pertain to our *thoughts*—thinking, judging, hoping, fearing, wishing, wondering, desiring, loving, hating, and intending. And some of them have to do with the ways in which we *sense*, or are *appeared* to. The first may be called *intentional* properties and the second may be called *sensible* properties. It was characteristic of philosophers in the empirical tradition to stress those self-presenting properties that are sensi-

---

[2]This concept of entailment will be discussed in more detail in Chapter 6.

ble and to neglect those that are intentional. But both types must be taken into consideration in any adequate theory of knowledge.

It is true, of course, that most of us have very little knowledge of our psychological makeup and that we are likely to accept oversimplified and false accounts of why it is we think and act as we do. But this fact is quite consistent with what we have said about self-presenting properties. For, although these properties may mislead us about *other* things, they are not a source of error about *themselves*.

The following objection is familiar in recent literature: "But contemporary science has established that we have no knowledge at all of our thoughts and indeed that we cannot even know *whether* we are thinking."[3] If science *had* established these things, then, of course, what we have been saying would be wrong. Upon investigation, however, it turns out that these are *not* things that "science has established." They are things that would be true if science were to tell us what certain philosophers of science think it ought to tell us.

SENSIBLE PROPERTIES

We now turn to those self-presenting properties that pertain to *sensing*, or *being appeared to*.

In the second of his *Meditations*, Descartes offers what he takes to be good reasons for doubting whether, on any occasion, he sees light, hears noise, or feels heat. Then he observes, "Let it be so, still it is at least quite *certain that it seems to me that* I see light, that I hear noise and that I feel heat."[4] This observation about seeming should be contrasted with what St. Augustine says, in his *Contra Academicos*, about appearing:

I do not see how the Academician can refute him who says: "I know that this *appears* white to me, I know that my hearing is delighted with this, I know that this has an agreeable odor, I know that this tastes sweet to me, I know that this feels cold to me." . . . I say this that, when a person tastes something, he can honestly swear that he knows it is sweet to his palate or the contrary, and that no trickery of the Greeks can dispossess him of that knowledge.[5]

Let us contrast Descartes' statement, "It seems to me that I see light," with St. Augustine's "I know that this appears white to me." For we have here two quite different uses of "appear" words.

[3]Those who speak in this way may refer to such writings as: Daniel Dennett, "Beyond Belief," in Andrew Woodfield, ed., *Thought and its Object: Essays on Intentionality* (Oxford: The Clarendon Press, 1982), pp. 1–95; and Stephen P. Stich, *From Folk Psychology to Cognitive Science* (Cambridge, MA: The MIT Press, 1983).

[4]E. S. Haldane and R. T. Ross, eds., *The Philosophical Works of Descartes*, I (London: Cambridge University Press, 1934) p. 153. (my italics)

[5]*Against the Academicians (Contra Academicos)*, Sister Mary Patricia Garvey, ed. (Milwaukee, WI: Marquette University Press. 1942), Paragraph 26; p. 68 of translation. (my italics)

"It seems to me that I see light," when uttered on any ordinary occasion, might be taken to be performing one or the other of two quite different functions. (1) The expression might be used simply to report one's belief; in such a case, "It seems to me that I see light" could be replaced by, "I believe that I see light." Taken in this way, the "seems" statement expresses what is self-presenting, but since it is equivalent to a belief-statement it does not add anything to the cases we have already considered. (2) "It seems to me"—or better, "It seems to *me*"—may be used not only to report a belief, but also to provide the speaker with a way out, a kind of hedge, in case the statement prefixed by, "It seems to me," should turn out to be false. This function of, "It seems," is thus the contrary of the performative use of, "I know," to which J. L. Austin had called attention. In saying, "I know," I give my hearers a kind of guarantee and, as Austin said, stake my reputation, but in saying "It seems to *me*," I play it safe, indicating that what I say carries no guarantee at all, and that anyone choosing to believe what I say does so at his or her own risk.[6]

But the word "appear" as it is used in St. Augustine's statement ("This appears white to me") performs a very different function: it describes a certain state of affairs that is not itself a belief. When "appear" is used in this descriptive, "phenomenological" way, then one may say consistently and without any incongruity, "That thing appears white to me in this light, but I know that it is really grey." One may also say, again, consistently and without any incongruity, "It appears white to me in this light and I know that, as a matter of fact, it *is* white."

The latter statement illustrates two points overlooked by many contemporary philosophers, the first being that in such a statement, "appear" cannot have the hedging use just referred to, for it it did, the statement would be incongruous (which it is not). The second part ("I know that it is white") would provide a guarantee which the first part ("This appears white") withholds. The second point is that the descriptive, phenomenological use of "appears" is not restricted to the description of *illusory experiences*. Merely by varying the state of the perceiving subject or the state of the intervening medium, or by varying other conditions of observation, we may also vary the ways in which the things that are perceived will appear to us. And "appear"-words *may* be used to describe such ways of appearing.

If, for any such characteristic F, I can justify a claim to knowledge by referring to something that is *appearing* F (by saying of the wine that it now *looks* red or *tastes* sour to me), where the verb and adverb are intended in the descriptive, phenomenological sense just indicated, then the *appearing* in question is self-presenting. The claim that I thus justify, by saying of something that it appears F, may be the claim that the thing *is* F, but, as we

[6]J. L. Austin discussed this use of "seems" in considerable detail in his posthumous *Sense and Sensibilia* (Oxford: The Clarendon Press, 1962). Compare the essay "Other Minds" in Austin's *Philosophical Papers* (Oxford: The Clarendon Press, 1961), pp. 44–84.

have seen, it may also be some other claim. To the question "What justification do I have for thinking that something now *looks* red to me or *tastes* sour?" I could reply only by reiterating that something does now look red or taste sour.

Strictly speaking, "The *wine* tastes sour to me," and "*something* looks red to me," do not express what is self-presenting in our sense of this term. For the first statement implies that there *is* a certain thing—namely, the wine— that I am tasting, and the second statement implies that there *is* a certain external thing that is appearing red to me. But, "I am tasting wine," and, "There is a certain external thing that is appearing red to me," do not express what is self-presenting. What justifies me in thinking that I am tasting wine is *not* simply the fact that I am tasting wine, and what justifies me in thinking that a certain thing is appearing red to me (and that I am not, say, merely suffering from a hallucination) is not simply the fact that a certain thing *is* appearing red to me. To arrive at what is self-presenting in these cases, we must remove the reference to the external thing—to the wine in, "The wine tastes sour to me," and to the appearing thing in, "That thing appears red to me." This, however, is very difficult to do, since our language was not developed for any such philosophical purpose.

Do we have ground for doubting the evident character of what is expressed by statements about appearing? Doubts have been raised in recent years and we should consider these briefly.

SOME MISCONCEPTIONS ABOUT APPEARING

There are *some* descriptive appear-statements that do not express what is self-presenting—for example, "She looks just the way her uncle did 15 years ago." If we describe a way of appearing by *comparing* it with the way in which some physical thing happens to have appeared in the past or with the way in which some physical thing is thought normally to appear, then the justification for what we say about the way of appearing will depend in part upon the justification for what we say about the physical thing; and what we say about the physical thing will not now be self-presenting.

It has been argued, however, that the types of appear-statements we have just been considering *also* involve some comparison with previously experienced objects, and, hence, that what they express can never be said to be self-presenting. It has been suggested, for example, that if I say, "This appears white," then I am making a "comparison between a present object and a formerly seen object."[7] What justification is there for saying this?

It is true that the expression, "appears white," may be used to abbreviate, "appears the way in which white things normally appear." But this fact

[7] Hans Reichenbach, *Experience and Prediction* (Chicago, IL: University of Chicago Press, 1938), p. 176.

should not prevent us from seeing that things may also be just the other way around: "white thing" may be used to abbreviate, "thing having the color of things that normally appear white." The expression, "appear white," as it is used in the latter sentence, is *not* used to abbreviate, "appear the way in which white things normally appear." For in saying that "white thing" may be used to abbreviate, "thing having the color of things that normally appear white," we are *not* saying simply that "white thing" may be used to abbreviate, "thing having the color of things which ordinarily appear the way in which *white things* normally appear." Therefore, when we say that "white thing" may be used to abbreviate, "thing having the color of things that ordinarily appear white," the point of "appear white" is not to *compare* a way of appearing with anything. Using, "appears white," in this way, we may say, significantly and without redundancy, "Things that *are* white normally *appear* white." And this is the way in which we should interpret, "This appears white to me," in the quotation above from St. Augustine. More generally, it is in terms of this descriptive, noncomparative use of our other "appear" and "seem" words (including "looks," "tastes," "sounds," and the like) that we are to interpret those appear-statements that are said to be self-presenting.

But philosophers have offered still other arguments to show that appear-words cannot be used in this noncomparative way. Each of the following three arguments, I believe, is quite obviously invalid.

(1) The first argument may be summarized in this way. "(a) Sentences such as, 'This appears white,' are 'parasitical upon' sentences such as, 'This *is* white'; that is to say, in order to understand, 'This appears white,' one must *first* be able to understand, 'This is white.' Therefore (b) 'This appears white' ordinarily means the same as, 'This appears in the way in which white things ordinarily appear,' Hence (c) 'This is white' *cannot* be used to mean the same as, 'This is the sort of thing that ordinarily appears white,' where 'appears white' is used in the way you have just described. And so (d) there is no clear sense in which what is expressed by, 'This appears white,' can be said to be self-presenting."

There is an advantage in thus making the argument explicit. For to see that the conclusion (d) does not follow from the premise (a), we have only to note that (c) does not follow from (d). From the fact that a linguistic expression is ordinarily used in one way, it does not follow that that expression may not also sometimes be used in another way. And so even if the linguistic hypothesis upon which the argument is based were true, the conclusion does not follow from the premise.

(2) The following is a more serious argument: "(a) If the sentence, 'I am appeared white to' does not express a comparison between a present way of appearing and anything else, then the sentence is completely empty and says nothing at all about a present way of appearing. But (b) if, 'I am appeared white to,' expresses what is certain, then it cannot assert a com-

parison between a present way of appearing and anything else. Therefore, (c) either 'I am appeared white to' is empty or it does not express what is certain."

Here the difficulty lies in the first premise. It may well be true that, if an appear-sentence is to communicate anything to another person, then it must assert some comparison of things. Thus if I wish *you* to know the way in which I am appeared to now, I must relate this way of being appeared to with something that is familiar to you. ("Describe the taste? It's something like the taste of a mango.") Two different questions have been confused here. One is this: (A) "If you are to understand me when I say something about the way in which I am appeared to, must I be comparing that way of appearing with the way in which some object, familiar to you, happens to appear?" And the second question is, more simply: (B) "Can I apprehend the way in which I am now appeared to without thereby supposing, with respect to some object, that the way I am being appeared to is the way in which that object sometimes appears or has appeared?" The question that we have been concerned with is (B), not (A). From the fact that question (A) must be answered negatively, it does not follow that question (B) must also be answered negatively.

The argument, moreover, presupposes an absurd thesis about the nature of thought or predication. This thesis might be expressed by saying that "all judgments are comparative." To see that this is absurd, we have only to consider more carefully what it says. It tells us that in order to believe, with respect to any particular thing x, that x has a certain property F, one must *compare* x with some other thing y and thus assert or believe of x that it has something in common with the other thing y. But clearly, we cannot derive "x is F" from "x resembles y" unless, among other things, we can believe *noncomparatively* that y is F.

(3) Still another argument designed to show that appear-statements cannot express what is certain, may be put as follows: "(a) In saying, 'Something appears white,' you are making certain assumptions about language; you are assuming, for example, that the word, 'white,' or the phrase, 'appears white,' is being used in the way in which you have used it on other occasions, or in the way in which other people have used it. Therefore (b), when you say, 'This appears white,' you are saying something, not only about your present experience, but also about all of these other occasions. But (c), what you are saying about these other occasions is not certain. And therefore (d), 'This is white' does not express what is certain."

The false step in this argument is the inference from (a) to (b). We must distinguish the belief that a speaker has about the *words* he is using from the belief that he is using those words to express. What holds true for the former need not hold true for the latter. A Frenchman, believing that "potatoes" is English for apples, may use, "There are potatoes in the basket," to express the belief that there are apples in the basket; from the fact that he has a mistaken belief about "potatoes" and "apples," it does not follow that he has a mistaken belief about potatoes and apples. Similarly, it may be that what a man believes about his own use of the expression, "appears white," is something that is not certain for him—indeed what he believes about his own language may even be false and unreasonable; but from these facts it does not follow that what he intends to assert when he utters, "This appears white to me," is something that cannot be certain.[8]

THE PROBLEM OF THE SPECKLED HEN

We consider finally what is sometimes called "the problem of the speckled hen."[9]

Consider the visual sensation that is yielded by a single glance at a speckled hen. The sensation may be said to contain many speckles. One may ask therefore, "*How many* speckles are there?" If we judge, say, that the sensation contains 48 speckles, we may very well be mistaken: perhaps there are a few more speckles or a few less. Yet our judgment is a judgment about the nature of the sense-datum—or about the nature of the way we sense. The fact that such a judgment may be mistaken would seem to be in conflict with our view according to which the nature of what we sense is self-presenting and therefore a source of certainty.

The example is clearly not an isolated one. Most presentations (for instance, those yielded by the marks on this piece of paper or by the leaves outside the window) are similarly multiplex. The problem, therefore, is fundamental to the theory of knowledge.

Let us recall what we said about the nature of self-presentation: if a property is self-presenting, then every property that it entails includes the property of thinking. This means that a self-presenting property is a property that is relatively simple and easy to grasp. Now the property of containing 48 speckles *entails* the property of being a speckle (for whoever believes something to have the property of containing 48 speckles also believes something to have the property of being a speckle). But the property of having 48 speckles does not *include* the property of being a speckle (one can *have* 48 speckles without thereby *being* a speckle). Hence the property of having 48 speckles is not a self-presenting property. And therefore the experience involved in looking at a speckled hen is not inconsistent with what we have said about self-presenting properties and certainty.

In the following chapter we turn to another source of certainty.

[8]For a further defense of this way of looking at appearing, compare John Pollock, *Knowledge and Justification* (Princeton, NJ: Princeton University Press, 1974), pp. 71–79.

[9]This problem was suggested to A. J. Ayer by Gilbert Ryle. See Ayer's *The Foundations of Empirical Knowledge* (New York: The Macmillan Company, 1940), p. 124ff. The example of the speckled hen was proposed by H. H. Price in his review of Ayer's book in *Mind*, Vol. L (1941), pp. 280–288. A discussion of other ways of dealing with the problem may be found in "The Problem of the Speckled Hen," by Roderick M. Chisholm, *Mind*, Vol. LI (1942), pp. 368–373.

CHAPTER 4

The A Priori

"There are also two kinds of truths: those of reasoning and those of fact. The truths of reasoning are necessary, and their opposite is impossible. Those of fact, however, are contingent, and their opposite is possible. When a truth is necessary, we can find the reason by analysis, resolving the truth into simpler ideas and simpler truths until we reach those that are primary." [Leibniz, *Monadology* 33]

AXIOMS

There are propositions that are necessarily true and such that, once one understands them, one *sees* that they are true. Such propositions have traditionally been called *a priori*. Leibniz remarks, "You will find a hundred places in which the scholastic philosophers have said that these propositions are evident, from their terms, as soon as they are understood."[1]

If we say of an *a priori* proposition, that, "once you understand it then you see that it is true," then we must take the term "understand" in a

[1]G. W. Leibniz, *New Essays Concerning Human Understanding*, translated and edited by Peter Remnant and Jonathan Bennett (New York: Cambridge University Press, 1982), Book IV, Ch. 7. Compare Alice Ambrose and Morris Lazerowitz, *Fundamentals of Symbolic Logic* (New York: Holt, Rinehart and Winston, Inc., 1962), p. 17. "A proposition is said to be true *a priori* if its truth can be ascertained by examination of the proposition alone or if it is deducible from propositions whose truth is so ascertained, and by examination of nothing else. Understanding the words used in expressing these propositions is sufficient for determining that they are true."

somewhat rigid sense. You could not be said to "understand" a proposition, in the sense intended, unless you can grasp *what* it is for that proposition to be true. The properties or attributes that the proposition implies—those that would be instantiated if the proposition were true—must be properties or attributes that you can conceive or grasp. To "understand" a proposition, in the sense intended, it is not enough merely to be able to say what *sentence* in your language happens to express that proposition. The proposition must be one that you have contemplated and reflected upon.

One cannot *accept* a proposition, in the sense in which we have been using the word "accept," unless one also *understands* that proposition. We might say, therefore, that an *a priori* proposition is one such that, if you accept it, then it becomes certain for you. (For, if you accept it, then you understand it, and, as soon as you understand it, it becomes certain for you.) This account of the *a priori*, however, would be at once too broad and too narrow. It would be too broad in that it also applies to what is self-presenting, and what is self-presenting is not necessarily true. It would be too narrow in that it does not hold of all *a priori* propositions. We know some *a priori* propositions on the basis of others, and these propositions are not themselves such that, once they are understood, then they are certain.

Let us begin by trying to characterize more precisely those *a priori* propositions that are not known on the basis of any other *a priori* propositions.

Leibniz said that these propositions are "the first illuminations." He wrote, "The immediate awareness of our existence and of our thoughts furnishes us with the first *a posteriori* truths, or truths of fact, i.e., *the first experiences*, while identical propositions embody the first *a priori* truths, or truths of reason, i.e., *the first illuminations*. Neither admits of proof, and each may be called *immediate*."[2]

The traditional term for those *a priori* propositions which are "incapable of proof" is *axiom*. Thus Frege wrote, "Since the time of antiquity an axiom has been taken to be a thought whose truth is known without being susceptible by a logical chain of reasoning."[3] In *one* sense, of course, every true proposition h is capable of proof, for there will always be other true propositions from which we can derive h by means of some principle of logic. What did Leibniz and Frege mean, then, when they said that an axiom is "incapable of proof"?

The answer is suggested by Aristotle. An axiom, or "basic truth," he said, is a proposition "which has no other proposition prior to it"; there is no proposition which is "better known" than it is.[4] And what does "better known" mean? Perhaps this: of two propositions both of which are known by a subject S, one is better known than the other provided only that S is

---

[2]*New Essays Concerning Human Understanding*, Book IV, Ch. 9.

[3]Gottlob Frege, *Kleine Schriften* (Hildesheim: Georg Olms (Verlagsbuchhandlung, 1967), p. 262.

[4]*Posterior Analytics*, Book I, Ch. 2.

more justified in accepting the one than in accepting the other. Hence, if an axiomatic proposition is one such that no other proposition is better known than it is, then it is one that is certain. (It will be recalled that we characterized *certainty* by saying this: a proposition *h* is *certain* for a person S, provided that *h* is evident for S and provided that, for every proposition *i*, believing *h* is at least as justified for S as believing *i*.) Hence Aristotle said that an axiom is a "primary premise." Its ground does not lie in the fact that it is seen to follow from *other* propositions. Therefore we cannot prove such a proposition by making use of any premises that are "better known" than it is. (By "a proof," then, Aristotle, Leibniz, and Frege meant more than "a valid derivation from premises that are true.")

Let us now try to say what it is for a proposition to be an *axiom*:

D1   h is an axiom = Df   h is necessarily such (i) it is true and (ii) for every S, if S accepts h, then h is certain for S

The following propositions among countless others may be said to be *axioms* in our present sense of the term:

> If some men are Greeks, then some Greeks are men.
> If Jones is ill and Smith is away, then Jones is ill.
> The sum of 5 and 3 is 8.
> The product of 4 and 2 is 8.
> All squares are rectangles.

These propositions are axiomatic in the following sense for those people who *do* consider them:

D2   h is *axiomatic* for S = Df   (i) h is an axiom and (ii) S accepts h.

We have assumed that any conjunction of axioms is itself an axiom. But it does not follow from this assumption that any conjunction of propositions which are axiomatic *for* a subject S is itself axiomatic for S. If two propositions are axiomatic for S and if S does not accept their conjunction, then the conjunction is not axiomatic for S. (Failure to accept their conjunction need not be a sign that S is unreasonable. It may be a sign merely that the conjunction is too complex an object for S to grasp.)

Our knowledge of what is axiomatic is a subspecies of our *a priori* knowledge, that is to say, some of the things we know *a priori* are *not* axiomatic in the present sense. They are *a priori* but they are not what Aristotle called "primary premises."

What would be an example of a proposition that is *a priori* for S but not axiomatic for S? Consider the last two axioms on our list above, i.e.,

> The sum of 5 and 3 is 8.
> The product of 4 and 2 is 8.

Let us suppose that their conjunction is also an axiom and that S accepts this conjunction; therefore the conjunction is axiomatic for S. Let us suppose further that the following proposition is axiomatic for S:

> If the sum of 5 and 3 is 8 and the product of 4 and 2 is 8, then the sum of 5 and 3 is the product of 4 and 2.

We will say that, if, in such a case, S accepts the proposition that the sum of 5 and 3 is the product of 4 and 2, then that proposition is *a priori* for S. Yet the proposition may not be one which is such that it is certain for anyone who accepts it. It may be that one can consider *that* proposition without thereby seeing that it is true.

There are various ways in which we might now attempt to characterize this broader concept of the *a priori*. We might say, for example, "You know a proposition *a priori* provided you accept it and provided it is implied by propositions that are axiomatic for you." But this would imply that *any* necessary proposition that you happen to accept is one that you know *a priori* to be true. (Any necessary proposition *h* is implied by any axiomatic proposition *e*. Indeed, any necessary proposition *h* is implied by *any* proposition *e*—whether or not *e* is axiomatic and whether or not *e* is true or false. For if *h* is necessary, then it is necessarily true that, for any proposition *e*, either *e* is false or *h* is true. And to say, "*e* implies *h*," is to say it is necessarily true that either *e* is false or *h* is true.) *Some* of the necessary propositions that we accept may *not* be propositions that we know *a priori*. They may be such that, if we know them, we know them *a posteriori*—on the basis of authority. Or they may be such that we cannot be said to know them at all.

To capture the broader concept of the *a priori*, we might say that a proposition is known *a priori* provided it is axiomatic that the proposition follows from something that is axiomatic. Let us put the matter this way:

D3   *h* is known *a priori* by S = Df   There is an *e* such that (i) *e* is axiomatic for S, (ii) the proposition, *e* implies *h*, is axiomatic for S, and (iii) S accepts *h*

We may add that a person knows a proposition *a posteriori* if he knows the proposition but does not know it *a priori*.

We may assume that what is thus known *a priori* is evident. But the *a priori*, unlike the axiomatic, need not be certain. This accords with St. Thomas's observation that "those who have knowledge of the principles [i.e., the axioms] have a more certain knowledge than the knowledge which is through demonstration."[5]

Is this account too restrictive? What if S derives a proposition from a set

---

[5]Thomas Aquinas, *Exposition of the Posterior Analytics of Aristotle*, tr. Pierre Conway (Quebec: M. Doyon, 1952), Book II, Lecture 20, No. 4, (pp. 427–428).

of axioms, not by means of one or two simple steps, but as a result of a complex proof, involving a series of interrelated steps? If the proof is formally valid, then shouldn't we say that S knows the proposition *a priori*?

I think that the answer is no. Complex proofs or demonstrations, as John Locke pointed out, have a certain limitation. They take time. The result is that the "evident lustre" of the early steps may be lost by the time we reach the conclusion: "In long deductions, and the use of many proofs, the memory does not always so readily retain." Therefore, he said, demonstrative knowledge "is more imperfect than intuitive knowledge."[6]

Descartes also noted that memory is essential to demonstrative knowledge. He remarks in *Rules for the Direction of the Mind* that, if we can *remember* having deduced a certain conclusion step by step from a set of premises that are "known by intuition," then, even though we may not now recall each of the particular steps, we are justified in saying that the conclusion is "known by deduction."[7] But if, in the course of a demonstration, we must rely upon memory at various stages, thus using as premises contingent propositions about what we happen to remember, then, although we might be said to have "demonstrative knowledge" of our conclusion, in a somewhat broad sense of the expression "demonstrative knowledge," we cannot be said to have an *a priori* demonstration of the conclusion.

Of course, we may make mistakes in attempting to carry out a proof just as we may make mistakes in doing simple arithmetic. And one might well ask, How can this be, if the propositions we are concerned with are known *a priori*? Sometimes, as the quotation from Locke suggests, there has been a slip of memory. Perhaps we are mistaken about just *what* the propositions are that we proved at an earlier step—just as, in doing arithmetic, we may mistakenly think we have carried the 2 or we may pass over some figure having thought that we included it or we may inadvertently include something twice. And there are also occasions when we may just seem to get the *a priori* proposition wrong. In my haste I say to myself, "9 and 6 are 13," and then the result will come out wrong. But when I do this, I am not really considering the proposition that 9 and 6 are 13. I may just be considering the formula, "9 and 6 are 13," which sounds right at the time and not considering at all the proposition that that formula is used to express.

We have said what it is for a proposition to be known *a priori* by a given subject. But we should note, finally, that propositions are sometimes said to be *a priori* even though they may not be known by anyone at all. Thus Kant held that "mathematical propositions, strictly so called, are always judg-

[6]*Essay Concerning Human Understanding*, Book IV, Chap. 2, Sec. 7.

[7]See *The Philosophical Works of Descartes*, ed. E. S. Haldane and G. R. T. Ross, I (London: Cambridge University Press, 1934), p. 8. Some version of Descartes' principle should be an essential part of any theory of evidence. Compare Norman Malcolm's suggestion: "If a man previously had grounds for being sure that *p*, and now remembers that *p*, but does not remember what his grounds were," then he "*has* the same grounds he previously had." *Knowledge and Certainty* (Englewood Cliffs, NJ: Prentice-Hall, Inc., 1963), p. 230.

ments *a priori*."[8] In saying this, he did not mean to be saying merely that mathematical propositions are necessarily true; he was saying something about their epistemic status and something about the way in which they could be known. Yet he could not have been saying that all mathematical propositions are known or even believed, by someone or other, to be true for there are propositions of mathematics that no one knows to be true and there are propositions of mathematics that no one has ever even considered. What would it be, then, to say that a proposition might be *a priori* even though it has not been considered by anyone? I think the answer can only be that the proposition is one that *could* be known *a priori*. In other words:

D4   *h* is *a priori* = Df   It is possible that there is someone for whom *h* is known *a priori*

This definition allows us to say that a proposition may be "objectively *a priori*"— "objectively" in that it is *a priori* whether or not anyone knows it *a priori*.

Our definitions are in the spirit of several familiar dicta concerning the *a priori*. Thus, we may say, as Kant did, that necessity is a mark of the *a priori*—provided we mean by this that, if a proposition is *a priori*, then it is necessary.[9] For our definitions assure us that whatever is *a priori* is necessarily true.

The definitions also enable us to say, as St. Thomas did, that these propositions are "manifest through themselves."[10] For an axiomatic proposition is one such that, once it is reflected upon or considered, then it is certain. What a given person knows *a priori* may not *itself* be such that, once it is considered, it is certain. But our definition enables us to say that, if a proposition is one that is *a priori* for you, then you can see that it follows from a proposition that is axiomatic.

Kant said that our *a priori* knowledge, like all other knowledge, "begins with experience" but that, unlike our *a posteriori* knowledge, it does not "arise out of experience."[11] A priori knowledge may be said to "begin with experience" in the following sense: there is no *a priori* knowledge until some proposition is in fact contemplated and understood. Moreover the acceptance of a proposition that is axiomatic is sufficient to make that proposition an axiom for whoever accepts it. But *a priori* knowledge does not "arise out of experience." For, if a proposition is axiomatic or *a priori*

[8]Immanuel Kant, *Critique of Pure Reason*, Norman Kemp Smith, trans. (London: Macmillan and Co., Ltd., 1933), p. 52.

[9]Compare *Critique of Pure Reason*, B4 (Kemp Smith edition, p. 44). But we should not assume that if a proposition is necessary and known to be true, then it is *a priori*.

[10]*Exposition of the Posterior Analytics of Aristotle* Book II, Lecture 20, No. 4 (pp. 427–428). Pierre Conway; Part I, Lecture 4, No. 10 (p. 26).

[11]*Critique of Pure Reason*, B1 (Kemp Smith edition, p. 41).

for us, then we have all the evidence we need to see that it is true. Understanding is enough; it is not necessary to make any further inquiry.

What Leibniz called "first truths *a posteriori*" coincide with what we have called "the self-presenting." And his "first truths *a priori*" coincide with what we have called "the *axiomatic*."[12]

ANALYSING THE PREDICATE OUT OF THE SUBJECT

The terms "analytic" and "synthetic" were introduced by Kant in order to contrast two types of *a priori* proposition. But Kant used the word "judgment" where we have been using "proposition."

An analytic judgment, according to Kant, is a judgment in which "the predicate adds nothing to the concept of the subject." If I judge that all squares are rectangles, then, in Kant's terminology, the concept of the subject of my judgment is the property of being square, and the concept of the predicate is the property of being rectangular. Kant uses the term "analytic," since, he says, the concept of the predicate helps to "break up the concept of the subject into those constituent concepts that have all along been thought in it."[13] Being square is the conjunctive property of being equilateral and rectangular; therefore the predicate of the judgment expressed by, "All squares are rectangular," may be said to "analyse out" what is contained in the subject. An analytic judgment, then, may be expressed in the form of an explicit redundancy, e.g., "Everything is such that if it is both equilateral and rectangular then it is rectangular." To deny such an explicit redundancy would be to affirm a *contradictio in adjecto*, for it would be to judge that there are things which both have and do not have a certain property—in the present instance, that there is something that both is and is not rectangular. Hence, Kant said that "the common principle of all analytic judgments is the law of contradiction."[14]

What did Kant mean when he said that, in an analytic judgment, the predicate may be "analysed out" of the subject?

Consider the sentence:

(1)   All squares are rectangles.

What this sentence expresses may also be put as:

(2)   Everything that is an equilateral thing and a rectangle is a rectangle.

[12]Compare Franz Brentano, *The True and the Evident* (London: Routledge & Kegan Paul, 1966), p. 130ff.

[13]*Critique of Pure Reason*, A7; Norman Kemp Smith translation, p. 48.

[14]*Prolegomena to Any Future Metaphysics*, (La Salle, IN: The Open Court Publishing Company, 1933), Sec. 2 (p. 15).

Sentence(2) expresses a paradigm case of a proposition in which the predi-cate-concept (expressed by "a rectangle") may be said to be analysed out of the subject-concept (expressed by "an equilateral thing and a rectangle"). The subject-concept is broken up into two constituent concepts, one of which is the same as the predicate concept.

The following sentence, which is logically equivalent to (2), does not express a proposition in which the predicate-concept may be said to be "analysed out" of the subject concept:

(3)　　　Everything that is a square and a rectangle is a rectangle

In this case, the subject-concept (expressed by "a square and a rectangle") is not broken up into two "constituent concepts." The concept expressed by "square" includes that expressed by "rectangle." But in the earlier proposi-tion(2), the concept expressed by "equilateral thing" does not include that expressed by "rectangle."

Let us now try to say precisely what Kant meant by saying that the predicate-concept of an analytic judgment may be "analysed out" of the subject-concept.

DEFINITION OF ANALYTIC PROPOSITION

Kant's term "judgment" is ambiguous, for it may be taken to refer either (a) to the *act* of judging or (b) to that proposition which may be said to be the *object* of judging. Let us take the term in the second sense.

What, then, is an analytic proposition—in that sense of "analytic" that was singled out by Kant? To answer the question, let us recall our concept of *entailment*:

D5　　　The property of being F entails the property of being G = Df　　　Believ-ing something to be F includes believing something to be G

Property entailment may thus be distinguished from property implication:

D6　　　The property of being F implies the property of being G = Df　　　The property of being F is necessarily such that if something exemplifies it then something exemplifies the property of being G

We have said that a property P *includes* a property Q provided only that P is necessarily such that whatever has it also has Q. We may now introduce an abbreviation:

D7　　　P is conceptually equivalent to Q = Df　　　Whoever conceives P conceives Q, and conversely

And now we may say what an analytic proposition is:

D8   The proposition that all F's are G's is analytic = Df   The property of
         being F is conceptually equivalent to a conjunction of two properties, P and
         Q, such that: (i) P does not imply Q, (ii) Q does not imply P, and (iii) the
         property of being G is conceptually equivalent to Q

The definiens may be said to tell us the sense in which, as Kant put it, the
predicate of an analytic proposition may be "analyzed out" of the subject.
     The following gives us the sense in which Kant understood "*synthetic
proposition*":

D9   The proposition that all F's are G's is synthetic = Df   The proposition
         that all F's are G's is not analytic

THE SYNTHETIC A PRIORI

Kant raised the question: Is there a synthetic *a priori*? In other words, are
there synthetic propositions that can be known *a priori* to be true?
     Unfortunately many contemporary philosophers who have discussed
this question have taken "synthetic *a priori*" much more broadly than Kant
took it and therefore much more broadly than the sense we have given
above. They have taken "analytic proposition" to mean the same as "proposition that is not synthetic." In their use, such propositions as, "Either it is
raining or it is not raining," and, "If all men are mortal and if Socrates is a
man, then Socrates is mortal," are called "analytic." But in considering
Kant's question, we will understand "analytic proposition" and "synthetic
proposition" in the ways in which he understood these expressions.
     The philosophical importance of the question is this: if a proposition can
be shown to be analytic, to be such that the predicate can be analysed out of
the subject, then it is a kind of redundancy; it is relatively trivial and one
may feel that it does not have any significant content. But this is not so of
synthetic propositions. Hence, if there are synthetic propositions that can
be known *a priori* to be true, then the kind of cognition that can be
attributed to reason alone may be considerably more significant.
     Let us consider, then, certain possible types of example of "the synthetic
a priori," so conceived.
     (1) One important candidate for the synthetic *a priori* is the knowledge
that might be expressed either by saying, "Being square includes having a
shape," or by saying, "Necessarily, everything that is square is a thing that
has a shape." The sentence, "Everything that is square is a thing that has a
shape," recalls our paradigmatic, "Everything that is square is a rectangle."
In the case of the latter sentence, we were able to "analyze the predicate out
of the subject": we replaced the subject term "square" with a conjunctive

term, "equilateral thing and a rectangle," and were thus able to express our proposition in the form:

> Everything that is an S and a P is a P

where the predicate may be said to be "analysed out of" the subject.

> The problem is to fill the blank in:
>
> Everything that is a ——— and a thing that has a shape is a thing that has a shape

in the appropriate way. But given our account of what it is to "analyse the predicate out of the subject," can we do this? I believe it is accurate to say that no one has ever *shown* how we can do this.

We might try filling the blank by, "either a square or a thing that does not have a shape," thus obtaining:

> Everything that is (a) either a square or a thing that does not have a shape and (b) a thing that has a shape is a thing that has a shape.

But the property of being square is not conceptually equivalent to the property expressed by, "either a square or a thing that does not have a shape." One could believe something to have the former property without believing it to have the latter. Therefore the proposed way of filling in the blank does not yield a proposition in which the predicate term may be said to be "analysed out" of the subject.

Other possible ways of filling the blank seem to have the same result.

The proposition, "Everything that is square has a shape," expresses what can be known *a priori* to be true. If we cannot find a way of showing that it is analytic (and, so far at least, we have not succeeded), then, it would seem, there is some presumption in favor of saying that it is synthetic *a priori*.

There are indefinitely many other sentences presenting essentially the same difficulties as, "Everything that is square has a shape." Examples are, "Everything red is colored"; "Everyone who hears something in C-sharp minor hears a sound." The sentences express what is known *a priori*, but no one has been able to show that they are analytic.[15]

(2) What Leibniz called the "disparates" furnish us with a second candidate for the synthetic *a priori*. These are closely related to the example just considered, but they involve problems that are essentially different. An example of a sentence concerned with disparates would be our earlier, "Being red excludes being blue," or, alternatively put, "Nothing that is red

---

[15]Compare C. H. Langford, "A Proof that Synthetic A Priori Propositions Exist," *Journal of Philosophy*, Vol. XLVI (1949), pp. 20–24.

is blue."[16] Philosophers have devoted considerable ingenuity to trying to show that, "Nothing that is red is blue," can be expressed as a sentence that is analytic, but so far as I have been able to determine, all of these attempts have been unsuccessful. Again, it is recommended that the reader try to reexpress, "Nothing that is red is blue," in such a way that the predicate may be "analysed out" of the subject in the sense we have described above.

(3) It has also been held, not without plausibility, that certain ethical sentences express what is synthetic *a priori*. Thus, Leibniz, writing on what he called the "supersensible element" in knowledge, said: "But to return to *necessary truths*, it is generally true that we know them only by this natural light, and not at all by the experience of the senses. For the senses can very well make known, in some sort, what is, but they cannot make known what *ought to be* or what could not be otherwise."[17] Or consider the sentence, "All pleasures, as such are intrinsically good, or good in themselves, whenever and wherever they may occur." If this sentence expresses something that is known to be true, then what it expresses must be synthetic *a priori*. To avoid this conclusion, some philosophers deny that sentences about what is intrinsically good, or good in itself, *can* be known to be true.[18] An examination of this view would involve us, once again, in the problem of the criterion.

(4) Kant held that the propositions of arithmetic are synthetic and *a priori*. In evaluating his view, we must, of course, understand "analytic" in the sense in which he intended it.

Does "$2 + 1 = 3$" express what Kant called an analytic proposition? If it does, the proposition is expressible in a way that satisfies D7, our definition of what it is for a proposition to be such that its predicate may be "analysed out of" its subject.

Perhaps the most natural way of putting "$2 + 1 = 3$" in the form of "All S are P" (or of "For every x, if x is S, then x is P") is this:

> For every x, if x is a set of 2 sets which are such that (a) they have no members in common, (b) one of them has exactly 2 members, and (c) the other has exactly 1, then x has exactly 3 members

This statement is of the proper form, but it does not satisfy D8, our definition of the Kantian sense of "analytic proposition." The predicate-concept—expressed by "having exactly 3 members"—is not conceptually equivalent to any of the conjuncts of the subject-concept. Therefore this way of reading the *a priori* truth expressed by "$2 + 1 = 3$," is not analytic in

---

[16]Compare John Locke, *Essay Concerning Human Understanding*, Book IV, Chap. 1, Sec. 7; Franz Brentano, *Versuch über die Erkenntnis* (Leipzig: Felix Meiner, 1970), pp. 9–10.

[17]Quoted from G. M. Duncan, ed., *The Philosophical Works of Leibnitz* (New Haven, CT: The Tuttle, Morehouse & Taylor Company, 1908, p. 162.

[18]Compare the discussion of this question in Chapters 5 and 6 in William Frankena, *Ethics*, Second Edition, Foundations of Philosophy Series (Englewood Cliffs, NJ: Prentice-Hall, Inc., 1973).

Kant's sense of "analytic." Other ways of putting the proposition into the form of "All S are P" are equally unsatisfactory. There is reason to believe, therefore, that Kant is right in saying that such truths are synthetic *a priori*.

"LINGUISTICISM"

It has been suggested that the sentences giving rise to the problem of the synthetic *a priori* are really "postulates about the meanings of words" and, therefore, that they do not express what is synthetic *a priori*. But if the suggestion is intended literally, then it would seem to betray the confusion between use and mention that we encountered earlier. A *postulate* about the meaning of the word "red," for example, or a sentence expressing such a postulate, would presumably mention the word "red." It might read, "The word 'red' may be taken to refer to a certain color," or perhaps, "Let the word 'red' be taken to refer to a certain color." But, "Everything that is red is colored," although it uses the words "red" and "colored," does not mention them at all. It is not the case, therefore, that, "Red is a color," refers only to words and the ways in which they are used.

A popular conception of the truths of reason is the view according to which they are essentially "linguistic." Many have said, for example, that the sentences formulating the truths of logic are "true in virtue of the rules of language" and, hence, that they are "true in virtue of the way in which we use words."[19] What could this possibly mean?

The two English *sentences*, "Being round includes being square," and, "Being rational and animal includes being animal," plausibly could be said to "owe their truth," in part, to the way in which we use words. If we used "being square" to refer to the property of being heavy and not to that of being square, then the first sentence (provided the other words in it had their present use) would be false instead of true. And if we used the word "and" to express the relation of disjunction instead of conjunction, then the second sentence (again, provided that the other words in it had their present use) would also be false instead of true. But as W. V. Quine has reminded us, "even so factual a sentence as 'Brutus killed Caesar' owes its truth not only to the killing but equally to our using the component words as we do."[20] Had "killed," for example, been given the use that "was survived by" happens to have, then, other things being the same, "Brutus killed Caesar" would be false instead of true.

It might be suggested, therefore, that the truths of logic and other truths of reason stand in this peculiar relationship to language: they are true

[19]See Anthony Quinton, "The *A Priori* and the Analytic," in Robert Sleigh, ed., *Necessary Truth* (Englewood Cliffs, NJ: Prentice-Hall, Inc., 1972), pp. 89–109.

[20]W. V. Quine, "Carnap and Logical Truth," *The Philosophy of Rudolf Carnap*, P. A. Schilpp, ed., (La Salle, IL: Open Court Publishing Co., 1963), p. 386.

"*solely* in virtue of the rules of our language" or *solely* in virtue of the ways in which we use words." But if we take the phrase "solely in virtue of" in the way in which it would naturally be taken, then the suggestion is obviously false.

To say of a sentence that it is true *solely* in virtue of the ways in which we use words or that it is true *solely* in virtue of the rules of our language, would be to say that the only condition that needs to obtain in order for the sentence to be true is that we use words in certain ways or that there be certain rules pertaining to the way in which words are to be used. But let us consider what conditions must obtain if the English sentence, "Being round excludes being square," is to be true. One such condition is indicated by the following sentence which we may call "T":

> The English sentence, "Being square excludes being round," is true, if and only if, being square excludes being round.

Clearly, the final part of T, the part following the second "if," formulates a necessary condition for the truth of the English sentence, "Being round excludes being square," but it refers to a relationship among properties and not to rules of language or ways in which we use words. Hence we cannot say that the *only* conditions that need to obtain in order for, "Being round excludes being square," to be true is that we use words in certain ways or that there be certain rules pertaining to the ways in which words are to be used; and therefore, the sentence cannot be said to be true solely in virtue of the ways in which we use words.

There would seem to be no clear sense, therefore, in which the *a priori* truths of reason can be said to be primarily "linguistic."[21]

---

[21] For further discussions of this question, see the selections in Paul K. Moser, ed., *A Priori Knowledge* (Oxford: Oxford University Press, 1987).

CHAPTER 5

The Evidence of the Senses

INTRODUCTION

It is primarily by means of perception that we know about the external things around us. Our senses, somehow, provide us with evidence about the things that stimulate them. No theory of knowledge can be taken seriously that is not adequate to this fact. Yet, the more we consider the nature of perceiving, the more difficult it is to understand the nature of perceptual evidence. Indeed it may be said that one has not fully understood the nature of the theory of knowledge until one has come to grips with the problem of the evidence of the senses.

The problem involves two types of question: (i) *descriptive* or "phenomenological" questions about those aspects of our experience that make perception a source of evidence about the external world; and (ii) *normative* questions about what it is that those aspects of our experience justify us in believing.

THE OBJECTS OF PERCEPTUAL VERBS

We may approach our subject somewhat indirectly by considering the grammatical objects of perceptual *verbs*—such verbs as "see," "hear," and perceive." These grammatical objects may be of three different kinds.

(1) Sometimes perceptual verbs take a very simple object, as in, "He sees a cat," and, "She hears a dog." This first use has no implications about what

the perceiver *believes* and it has no implications about the *knowledge* or *evidence* that he or she has. For we may consistently say, "He sees a dog but he doesn't think that it is a dog that he sees"; and similarly for, "She hears a cat."

(2) Sometimes the grammatical object of a perception verb is a "that"-clause, as in, "He sees that a cat is on the roof," and, "She hears that the dog is scratching at the door." This use, unlike the first, does have implications with respect to *belief* and also with respect to *knowledge*. If she hears that the dog is at the door, then she knows that the dog is there and thus also believes it.

(3) Sometimes the grammatical object is a "semi-complex" one that seems to fall between the simple grammatical object ("a cat," "a dog") and the propositional object ("that a cat is on the roof," "that the dog is scratching at the door"). Examples of such semi-complex objects are provided by, "He sees a cat sitting on the roof," and, "She hears the dog scratching at the door." This third use can be misleading, especially in writing on the philosophy of perception.

Such a statement as, "He sees a cat on the roof," is relatively simple and straightforward. It is sometimes said that such statements provide us with no ground for philosophical puzzlement: they simply refer to a familiar kind of causal process which is of concern to particular sciences but not to philosophy.[1] But a mere description of the causal process has no implications about the perceiver's immediate experience or about what he is justified in believing. And for precisely this reason it does not provide us with what we are looking for.

To get at the nature of perceptual evidence, we must look further at those statements in which the perceptual verb has a complex grammatical object, such statements as, "He perceives that a cat is on the roof," and, "She hears that the dog is scratching at the door." Ordinarily, when we use our perception words in these ways, our statements commit us to what is affirmed in their subordinate "that"-clauses. "He perceives that a cat is on the roof" implies that there *is* a cat on the roof. And, "She hears a dog that is scratching at the door," implies that there *is* a dog that is scratching at the door. *Sometimes*, to be sure, we do not take our perception sentences to have such implications. We may say, "Well, *he* perceives that a cat is there, but obviously he is hallucinating once again; he is always seeing some cat or another that isn't really there." But I suggest that, to avoid ambiguity, we renounce this type of use.

If this suggestion is followed, then, "He perceives that a cat is on the roof," will imply, in our use, that there is a cat on the roof. And, "She hears that the dog is scratching at the door," will imply that there is a dog scratch-

---

[1]Compare Alvin Goldman, "A Causal Theory of Knowing," reprinted in George S. Pappas and Marshall Swain, eds., *Essays on Knowledge and Justification* (Ithaca, NY: Cornell University Press, 1978), pp. 61–86; the quotation is on p. 69.

ing at the door. And when we talk this way, then we may, so to speak, take the subject-term out of the "that"-clause and put it out in front. In other words, we may move from the *de dicto* locution:

> He perceives that there is a cat on the roof.

to the *de re* locution:

> A cat on the roof is perceived by him to be a cat on the roof

This is a move we cannot make in the case, "He believes that there is a cat on the roof," and, "He takes there to be a cat on the roof."

How, then, are we to describe the state of the person who is hallucinating—the person of whom one may be tempted to say, "*He* perceives that a cat is there, but obviously he is hallucinating once again"? The simplest procedure might be to say, "He *thinks* he perceives that a cat is there," or, "He *believes* that he perceives that a cat is there." An alternative would be, "He *takes* something to be a cat."

BEING APPEARED TO

The principal source of our philosophical problem lies in the fact that perception is inextricably bound up with *appearing*—with being appeared to in some way. The person who perceives that there is a tree before him *takes* there to be a tree. And when one takes there to be a tree (when one thinks that one perceives a tree), then one is appeared to in a certain way and one believes that *what* it is that is appearing in that way is a tree. In the case of the person who is hallucinating, we may say that, although he is *appeared to* in a certain way, there is nothing that is *appearing* to him in that way. We may characterize *perceptual taking* as follows and then define *perceiving* in terms of taking:

> S *takes* there to be an F = Df   (1) S is appeared — to; (2) it is evident to S that he is appeared — to; and (3) S believes that there is only one thing that appears — to him and that that thing is F

> S *perceives* that there is an F = Df   (1) There is an F that is appearing in a certain way to S; (2) S takes there to be an F that is appearing to him in that way; and (3) it is evident to S that an F is appearing to him in that way

"A perceives that there is an F," so defined, will imply, "S knows that there is an F."

If you perceive that there is a tree before you, then you believe that your perceptual experience is an experience of a tree—or, in our terminology, you think you are appeared to by a tree. It would be misleading to call the appearance the "*object*" of perception. But it would be accurate to say that, it is *by means of* what you know about the appearance, that you apprehend the object of perception. The philosophical problem of perceptual evidence turns on this question: how is it possible for appearances to provide us with information about the things of which they *are* appearances?

The difficulty has to do with what is sometimes called "perceptual relativity." The appearances that we sense are a function, not only of the nature of the things we perceive, but also of the conditions under which we perceive those things. To see that sense-appearances are a function of the conditions of observation, we have only to remind ourselves of this fact: whenever an external thing appears to us, then, merely by varying the conditions of observation and letting the external thing remain constant, we can vary the appearances that the thing presents.

Sextus Empiricus had cited these examples:

The same water which feels very hot when poured on inflamed spots seems lukewarm to us. And the same air seems chilly to the old but mild to those in their prime, and similarly the same sound seems to the former faint, but to the latter clearly audible. The same wine which seems sour to those who have previously eaten dates or figs seems sweet to those who have just consumed nuts or chickpeas; and the vestibule of the bathhouse which warms those entering from the outside chills those coming out.[2]

This completes our discussion of the *descriptive* questions involved in explicating the evidence of the senses.

THE NORMATIVE QUESTIONS

If appearances are so variable and if we perceive the things around us by means of the appearances that they present to us, then how can such perception provide us with any evidence about the external world? This question takes us to our *normative* questions.

The third clause in our definition of perceiving ("It is evident to S that he is appeared to in that way") is a *normative* expression, for it contains the epistemic locution, "It is evident to S that . . ." The normative epistemological problem is analogous to the problem we encounter in ethics or moral philosophy when we attempt to describe the conditions under which such expressions as, "It is right that . . ." and, "It is intrinsically good that . . ." may be applied. We want to find a *criterion* stating a non-normative situation that warrants the assertion of a normative statement—a non-

[2]*Outlines of Pyrrhonism*, Book I, Chap. 14; abridged from Vol. I of *Sextus Empiricus*, The Loeb Classical Library, pp. 55, 63, 65. Cf. K. Lykos, "Aristotle and Plato on 'Appearing,' "*Mind*, Vol. LXXIII (1964), pp. 496–514.

normative situation upon which, as it is sometimes said, a normative situation "supervenes."[3]

Thus we will look for criteria of this form:

So-and-so tends to make it evident to S that he is appeared to by an F

Such criteria will tell us something about the conditions under which S is *justified* in believing that there is an F. The conditions in question will not themselves be normative facts: they will be non-normative facts (say, being appeared to in certain ways) which constitute sufficient conditions for the existence of certain normative facts.

THREE TYPES OF PERCEPTUAL THEORY

One way to understand the normative questions about perceptual evidence is to consider three theories that we find in ancient Greek philosophy. The theories were concerned with the role of *appearances* (or the role of being *appeared to*) in the justification of perceptual belief. The first of these theories—"the *dogmatic* theory"—was "the theory of the evident perception" set forth by the Stoic, Chrysippus (279–206 B.C.); the second was "the *inductive* theory" developed by Sextus Empiricus (c. 150–250); and the third, which I will call "the *critical* theory," was the theory of the Academic skeptic, Carneades (c. 213–129 B.C.). The first two theories have some initial plausibility, but it is the theory of Carneades, I think, that is closest to the truth.

(1) The Dogmatic Theory

The question, then, is: How is it that appearances, which are dependent both upon internal and external conditions, can provide us with information about things that are external to us?

According to "the theory of the evident perception," the appearance presents us with *two* things—the appearance itself and the external thing that appears: there is a way of appearing that presents *itself* to the subject and also presents *another* thing to the subject—a thing that *appears* in a certain way to the subject. It was held that, whenever we have an evident

---

[3]Compare the following discussions of the normative aspect of the theory of knowledge: William Alston, "Conceptions of Epistemic Justification," *The Monist*, Vol. 68 (1985); Roderick Firth, "Are Epistemic Concepts Reducible to Ethical Concepts?" in Alvin Goldman and Jaegwon Kim, eds., *Values and Morals* (Dardrecht: D. Reidel, 1978) pp. 215–230; Richard Foley, *The Theory of Epistemic Rationality* (Cambridge, MA: Harvard University Press, 1986), Chapter 5: and John Pollock, *Contemporary Theories of Knowledge* (Totowa, NJ: Rowman & Littlefield, 1986), pp. 123–133.

perception, we can tell from the nature of the perceptual experience itself that the perception is veridical—that things are what we *take* them to be. The experience was said to be irresistable. "The perception, being plainly evident and striking, lays hold of us, almost by the very hair, as they say, and drags us off to assent, needing nothing else to help it to be thus impressive."[4] But, more important, it was said that the experience gives us a kind of guarantee.

Just what, then, is supposed to justify what? What is there about the *appearance* that presents the external object to us? And what is it about the *object* that the appearance makes evident to us about the object?

Chrysippus, the proponent of the dogmatic theory, suggested that the nature of the external thing can be "read off" from the nature of the appearances. When I have an evident perception, he said, the external thing "appears so true that it could not appear to me in the same way if it were false."[5] Hence the "dogmatic" criterion might be put in some such way as this:

> Being appeared to in such a way that, if one is appeared to in that way then one cannot resist believing that an F is appearing to one in that way, makes it evident that one is appeared to in that way by an F

What makes this view "dogmatic" is the fact that the criterion contains the guarantee "makes it evident that" rather than the more tentative "tends to make it evident that." (We will discuss these two concepts in more detail in the following chapter.)

Chrysippus suggests that the appearance that is yielded by a veridical perception could not be duplicated in an unveridical perception or in an hallucination. But this is contrary to what we know. For what the facts of perceptual relativity tell us is that there is no *logical* connection between the nature of any appearance, or way of being appeared to, and the nature of the object that serves to call up that appearance.

The dogmatic criterion of Chrysippus, then, does not allow us to say that the senses supply us with any information about things external to us. We must go further if we are to have a satisfactory account of the evidence of the senses.

(2) **The Inductive Theory**

The theory of "the commemorative perception" that was set forth by Sextus Empiricus was an "inductive" theory.

Sextus agrees with Chrysippus that our perceptual experience provides

[4]Quoted by Sextus Empiricus, "Against the Logicians," I, 257–258; Vol. II, pp. 137–139.

[5]Cicero uses these words in his *De Academica*, Vol. II, xi, p. 34; Cicero, *De Natura Deorum; Academica*, Loeb Classical Library (New York: G. P. Putnam's Sons, 1933), p. 511.

us with a *sign* of the independently existing external thing. But he rejects the dogmatism of Chrysippus: the nature of the appearance provides no *logical* guarantee of the nature of the object. Sextus points out, moreover, that normally we do not "read off" the nature of the object from the nature of the appearance—any more than we "read off" the nature of fire from the nature of smoke. Smoke signifies fire for us because we have made an induction that correlates smoke with fire: we have found in the past that smoke is generally accompanied by fire.[6] This much is quite obvious. But now Sextus goes on to take a further step.

One of the most astonishing things in the history of the theory of knowledge up to and including the present time is that most philosophers have failed to see how doubtful this step is.

Sextus says that the inductive correlation that we have made between smoke and fire gives us the clue to the relation between appearances and the external things that they make known to us. And he seems to suggest that we have made an inductive correlation between tree-appearances and external trees: we have found that tree-appearances are generally accompanied by the existence of external, physical trees. He concludes that the nature of an appearance may *make probable* some hypothesis about the nature of the external object. C. I. Lewis, addressing the same problem, says that "the given appearance is a valid *probability-index* of the objective property"; there are, according to Lewis, various "degrees of reliability" that appearances may have with respect to hypotheses about external objects.[7]

One might try to put the "inductive" criterion this way:

> If there is a way of appearing which is such that, more often than not, when S has been appeared to in that way an F has appeared to him, and if S is being appeared to in that way, then it is probable for S that he is perceiving an F

To see that there is something wrong with this account of perception, we have only to ask: what was the nature of those *earlier* experiences wherein we found that a tree-like appearance was accompanied by the apprehension of an external, physical tree? How was it made known to us *then* that there was a tree there? We are given no clear answers to this question. The inductive theory transfers the question to those earlier experiences

---

[6]Thus Sextus distinguished between (1) the "indicative" signs of Chrysippus, where one reads off the nature of the signified from the nature of the sign, and (2) the "commemorative signs" of the "empirical" physicians: a certain symptom signifies a certain disorder in virtue of the fact that we have experienced symptom and disorder together. See "Outlines of Pyrrhonism," Book II, Ch. X ("Concerning Sign") and Ch. XI ("Does Indicative Sign Exist?"); Loeb Library edition, Vol. I (Cambridge, MA: Harvard University Press, 1933) pp. 213–237.

[7]C. I. Lewis, "Professor Chisholm and Empiricism," *Journal of Philosophy*, Vol. XLV (1948), pp. 517–524; the quotations appear on p. 520. This article is reprinted in C. I. Lewis, *Collected Papers of C. I. Lewis* (Stanford, CA: Stanford University Press, 1970), pp. 317–325.

wherein we were able to correlate tree-appearances with the perception of external trees. And then it leaves the question unanswered.

I would say, therefore, that the "inductive" theory does not provide us with what we are looking for.

An inductive argument need not, of course, be enumerative. That is to say, it need not be of the form: "'Most A's are B's and x is an A' tends to make probable 'x is a B.'" But if any inductive argument tends to make it probable that one is appeared to by something that is F, then, presumably, the premises of the argument should include *some* evidence about external things. But where would S get *that* evidence? Once we try to answer this question, we see that we are left with our original problem. We had wanted to know just how it comes about that we have evidence concerning the nature of external things. We had assumed that, in the first instance, such evidence must arise out of perception. But the type of inductive theory now being considered tells us only how it is that, once we already have certain *prior evidence* about external things, perception can then go on to supply us with *additional* evidence about such things. And the theory does not tell us about the prior evidence.[8]

Yet perception *does* tell us something about the external world. Therefore there must be an alternative account of perceptual evidence.

(3) The Critical Theory

Carneades' critical theory has been expounded for us by Sextus Empiricus in his *Outlines of Pyrrhonism* and in his treatise, *Against the Logicians*.[9] Carneades says, in effect, that if a person takes something to be a tree, then, for that person, the proposition that there is a tree is *probable*. Carneades begins, then, in the same way that Sextus does. Where, then, does his view differ from the view of Sextus?

Sextus says that the probability of a perceptual taking is derived from an inductive correlation or frequency. But Carneades appeals to no such correlation. When he says that the object of the taking is probable, he does *not* say that this probability derives from any induction. And the reason for not saying this is clear: Carneades knows that we cannot make any inductive inferences about external things until we have some *perceptual data* about such things. And it follows from this that, if we are to have any positive justification for what we believe about the external world, our experience must provide us with a probability that is *not* derived from an induction.

It would miss the point to object, "But probability is, by definition, a matter involving inductive frequencies. You contradict yourself if you say

[8]A similar point may be made with respect to those theories that exhibit perceptual hypotheses as "constituting the best explanation" for our perceptual experiences. To show that such hypotheses *are* better explanations than others, one must appeal to additional evidence. But what is the source of that evidence?

[9]Vol. I, pp. 139–143, and Vol. II, pp. 67–103. Compare Charlotte L. Stough, *Greek Skepticism: A Study in Epistemology* (Berkeley, CA: University of California Press, 1969), esp. pp. 50–64.

that there is a kind of probable belief that has nothing to do with such frequencies." The sense of "probable" that we have used to express Carneades' view is, as we have said, quite different: it expresses a *normative* concept. To say that a proposition is probable for a given person, in this normative sense, is to say that the person has a certain positive justification for accepting that proposition. A proposition is *probable*, in this sense that, for a given person S, if and only if, S is more justified in accepting that proposition than he or she is in accepting its negation.

One of the things that Carneades was saying seems to have been this:

> Taking something to be F tends to make it probable that there is something one is taking to be F

Here, then, we have the beginnings of an answer to our question about perceptual evidence, "What aspect of our experience justifies what kind of belief about physical things?" The fact that the perceiver *takes* there to be a tree is a fact that "presents itself" to the perceiver: if he takes there to be a tree, then it is probable for him that he takes there to be a tree. And this intentional attitude, this taking, tends to make it probable that the taking has an actual object: it tends to make probable that there *is* in fact an external object upon which the taking is directed.

It should be noted that we have brought the quantifier from the inside to the outside of the intentional object of the "taking"-verb. What is probable for the perceiver is that there *is* something that he takes to be a tree.

We may go beyond this claim in two respects. We may say (1) that, under certain conditions, the perceptual taking yields, not only *probability*, but also *evidence* and (2) that *what* it tends to make evident is its own intentional object. In other words:

> Taking something to be F tends to insure the evidence of there being something that is F

This view was suggested by Meinong in 1906. He said, using a slightly different terminology from that used here, that perceptual judgments may have *presumptive evidence (Vermutungsevidenz)*: when one takes there to be a tree then the judgment that there *is* a tree that one is perceiving may have presumptive evidence. The qualification "presumptive" was intended to suggest that the judgment may have such evidence without thereby being *true*.[10] This view was subsequently developed further by H. H. Price. He made the following suggestion in his book, *Perception* (1933):

[10] A. Meinong, *Über die Erfahrungsgrundlagen unseres Wissens* (1910); see *Meinong Gesamt Ausgabe*, Vol. V (Graz: Akademische Druck- und Verlagsanstalt, 1973), pp. 438, 458–559. Compare his "Toward an Epistemological Assessment of Memory" (1886), reprinted in Roderick M. Chisholm and Robert J. Swartz, eds., *Empirical Knowledge: Readings from Contemporary Sources* (Englewood Cliffs, NJ: Prentice-Hall, Inc., 1973), pp. 253–269.

[T]he fact that a material thing is perceptually presented to the mind is *prima facie evidence* of the thing's existence and of its really having that sort of surface which it ostensibly has; . . . there is *some presumption in favour of* this, not merely in the sense that we do as a matter of fact presume it (which of course we do) but in the sense that we are entitled to do so.[11]

Price adds: "Clearly the principle is *a priori*: it is not the sort of thing we could learn by empirical generalization based upon observation of the material world."[12] (We will discuss in Chapter 6 the question of whether such principles can be *a priori*.)

The assumption is that, occasionally at least, the senses provide us with evidence pertaining to the existence of such things as trees, ships, and houses. The best answer to the question, "What is the nature of this evidence?" seems to be this: the fact that we are *appeared to* in certain ways *tends* to make it evident that there *is* an external thing that is appearing to us in those ways. And the fact that we *take* there to be a tree *tends* to make it *evident* for us that there is a tree that we perceive.

We turn, then, to the concept expressed by "tending to make evident."

[11]H. H. Price, *Perception* (New York: Robert M. McBride and Company, 1933), p. 185.
[12]Op. cit., p. 186.

CHAPTER 6

The Transfer of Justification

INTRODUCTION

Some propositions derive their epistemic status from other propositions. We make use of this fact when we calculate probabilities. From information about observed cases we determine the status of hypotheses about unobserved cases. Some propositions may derive their *evidence*—their status as being *evident*—from other propositions. Thus the proposition that I now see a sheep, for example, is evident for me and it derives its evidence from propositions about my present sense-experience and the conditions under which that experience occurs. And if there are propositions about the *past* that are evident for me, such propositions derive their evidence from propositions about the *present*—from propositions concerning what I take to be traces, relics, or memories of the past.

The explication of these relational epistemic concepts—the transfer of evidence and the transfer to probability—constitutes one of the most important and most difficult tasks of the theory of knowledge. And it is a topic that has been somewhat neglected in contemporary writings.

We will consider here two types of relational epistemic concepts—those that are merely *logical* and those that are *applied*. The logical concepts are illustrated by the relations expressed by, "e tends to make h evident," and, "e tends to make h probable." The applied concepts are illustrated by, "e makes h evident *for* a given subject S," and, "e makes h probable for S."

We begin with the transfer of evidence.

THE PROBLEM OF THE TRANSFER OF EVIDENCE

What are the relations that must obtain between two propositions if one of them is to be such that it *tends* to make the other evident? Many philosophers assume, apparently uncritically, that these relations may be characterized by reference to the logical principles of probability and induction. The following definition of the logical evidential relation is then presupposed:

e tends to make h evident = Df   e is necessarily such that it tends to provide h
with strong inductive support

But such a definition involves two serious difficulties.

(a) Our consideration of the evidence of the senses makes it clear that this type of definition does not include everything it should include. My present sense-experiences make it evident to me that I now see a sheep, but these experiences, as we saw in discussing the view of Sextus Empiricus, cannot be said to provide *inductive* support for the proposition that I see a sheep. So, too, for those present facts—if there are any—that tend to make it evident that it snowed here last night.

Therefore the above definition of tending-to-make-evident does not apply to all the cases to which it should apply.

(b) Presumably, if you are like most of the rest of us, you have very strong inductive support for the proposition that you will be alive next week. If we were to say that whatever has strong inductive support is evident, then we would have to say that it is now *evident* to you that you will be alive next week. But this conclusion would have disastrous results for the theory of knowledge. For if it happens to be true that you are going to be alive next week, and if you believe that you are, then the above definition would require us to say that you now *know* that you will be alive next week. But this is *not* one of those things that you can now be said to know.

Our earlier example may make the point more clearly. You know that you have walked today and you know that you had walked yesterday and the day before. But whatever your present evidence may be, you do not now *know* that you will walk tomorrow. If you were keeping statistical records of your walking in order to make a contribution to some scientific study, you would seriously compromise the investigation if you now submitted a report implying that you will have walked every day next week. It would not be rational to use such propositions about the future as *data*. The propositions have a *very* high degree of inductive support, but they cannot be included among the things that you now *know* to be true.

Therefore the above attempt to define, "e tends to make *h* evident," in terms of inductive support applies to cases to which it should not apply.

These points should help to make it clear why we need to distinguish *levels* of epistemic justification. The distinction between what is evident and what is not evident, as we have said, is not a mere quantitative distinction. It is qualitative like the distinction between being in motion and being at rest and like the distinction between having a conscious state that includes auditory sensations and having one that does not.

ENTAILMENT

To solve our problems we must make use of the concept of propositional *entailment*.

In discussing self-presenting properties, we said what it is for one property to *entail* another property. The property of being F, we said, *entails* the property of being G, provided only that believing something to be F includes believing something to be G. And one property may be said to *include* another property provided only that the first property is necessarily such that whatever has it also has the second.

Thus the property of believing there to be round squares entails the property of believing there to be things that are round, for one cannot believe that there are round squares without also believing that there are things that are round. If one property entails another, then the first property also *logically implies* the other; that is to say, the first property is necessarily such that if anything has it then something has the second. But one property may logically imply another property *without* thereby entailing that other property. The property of being greater than 7 logically implies the property of being greater than the square root of 49, but it does not entail that property. It is possible for someone to believe that something has the property of being greater than 7 without thereby believing that something has the property of being the square root of 49; for such a person may not have any idea that there *are* such things as square roots, much less *believe* that something is greater than the square root of 49.

This concept of property entailment has its analogue in the case of *propositions*. One proposition may be said to entail another provided only that accepting the first includes accepting the second.[1] Hence we may define propositional entailment this way:

D1   e entails h = Df   e is necessarily such that whoever accepts it accepts h

As in the case of properties, we may say that entailment includes logical implication, and that logical implication does not include entailment. If one

---

[1] It should be noted that the technical term "entails," in its application to propositions, is sometimes used in a slightly different way. If we wish to distinguish the present use from others, we could say that the concept here defined is that of *doxastic entailment*. The entailment relation that holds between properties could be called *attributional entailment*. The most thorough investigation of these topics is contained in Allen H. Renear, "Varieties of International Implication," Doctoral dissertation, Brown University, 1988.

proposition entails another, it also logically implies that other; but one proposition may logically imply another without entailing that other. The proposition that there are stones logically implies the proposition that 54 + 42 = 96, but it does not entail that proposition; you could accept the first without accepting the second.

This concept of entailment is of fundamental importance to the philosophy of mind and therefore also to the theory of knowledge. We will now see that it is essential to the theory of evidence.

TENDING TO MAKE EVIDENT

In saying what it is for one proposition to tend to make another evident, we will make use of the example that was discussed in the previous chapter: taking there to be a tree tends to make it evident that one perceives a tree. Our concern in the present chapter is not to defend this example but to say what it involves.

The relation of tending-to-make-evident is a logical relation between propositions. It is a relation which is such that, if it holds between two propositions, then it holds *necessarily* between those two propositions. And the applied relation of *making-evident* (the relation expressed by, "e makes h evident for S") is an application of this logical relation—an application of it *to* the body of evidence of a particular person. The *body of evidence* that you have—or, better, your *total evidence*—may be thought of as the set of all those propositions that are evident for you.

Suppose that you look out the window in an unfamiliar place and take something to be a tree. Then—since taking there to be a tree tends to make it evident that one perceives there to be a tree—your total evidence will be such that either (a) it also includes, "I perceive there to be a tree," or (b) it includes some special information about the conditions under which you take there to be a tree.

Let us first consider the case where your total evidence includes both, "I take there to be a tree," and, "I perceive there to be a tree." Consider now that proposition w which results from *subtracting*, "I perceive there to be a tree," from your total evidence. This proposition could *not* be anyone's total evidence. Anyone for whom *that* much is evident will also have additional evidence not included in w. We could say, therefore, that the conjunction of w and, "I take there to be a tree," is *evidentially incomplete* and that it could be *fulfilled* by, "I perceive there to be a tree."

What if, in the case envisaged, your total evidence does *not* include, "I perceive there to be a tree"? Then it will include evidence which would enable one to see *why* it is that, even though you take there to be a tree and even though taking there to be a tree tends to make it evident that one perceives there to be a tree, it is nevertheless *not* evident to you that you perceive there to be a tree. This further evidence might include, "I seem to recall that I have a perceptual disorder which leads me to take there to be trees when no trees are there."

We may define "tending to make evident" as follows:

D2   e tends to make h evident = Df   e is necessarily such that, if it is evident for someone x, then there is a w such that (i) w is evident for x, (ii) w&e cannot be anyone's total evidence, and (iii) w&e&h can be someone's total evidence

It will follow that, if e tends to make h evident, then e does not entail h. Hence no proposition tends to make itself evident: no proposition *derives* the evidence that it has from itself.

In the case where you take there to be a tree and it is *not* evident to you that you perceive there to be a tree, then one of the propositions that is evident for you may be said to *defeat* the tendency of taking-there-to-be-a-tree to make evident perceiving-there-to-be-a-tree. One such defeater is the proposition just cited, "I seem to recall that I have a perceptual disorder which leads me to take there to be trees when in fact no trees are there."

The relevant concept of *defeat* is this:

D3   d defeats e's tendency to make h evident = Df   e tends to make h evident; and d&e does not tend to make h evident

MAKING EVIDENT

Now we may consider the application of this logical relation to the evidence of a particular subject. Consider a person *for* whom taking there to be a tree makes it evident that he or she perceives there to be a tree. It will be evident to such person that he or she does take there to be a tree. And nothing that is evident to the person will *defeat* the tendency of taking-there-to-be-a-tree to make it evident that one perceives there to be a tree. That is to say, every proposition *d* that is evident to the person will be such that the conjunction of *d* and, "I take there to be a tree," tends to make evident, "I perceive there to be a tree."

We may now say what it is for one proposition to *make evident* another proposition for a particular subject S:

D4   e makes h evident for S = Df   (1) e is evident for S; (2) e tends to make whatever h entails evident; and (3) nothing that is evident for S defeats e's tendency to make h evident

We have seen that no proposition *tends* to make itself evident. The present definition has the consequence, then, that no proposition *makes* itself evident for anyone. And this consequence is as it should be, for no proposition can *derive* its evidence from itself. The point has been made clearly by James Van Cleve, "How could anything transmit evidence to itself? The prospect sounds circular at best (like a witness testifying in behalf of his own credibility), impossible at worst (like a man trying to improve his own net worth by borrowing money from himself)."[2] No proposition is included in its own evidence-makers.

We should note that, although nothing that e entails may be said, in the sense just defined, to be *made evident* by e, nevertheless if e is evident for S, then anything that e entails *is* also evident for S.

Our consideration of perceptual evidence, then, has enabled us to say what it is for one proposition that is evident for a person to derive its evidence from another proposition that is evident for that person. There are other epistemic relations that are similar to this. I suggest that we now have the clue to understanding these concepts. Let us consider just probability.

TENDING TO MAKE PROBABLE

The relation of tending-to-make-probable is one that holds necessarily between propositions. It may be expressed in a number of ways. For example, "e tends to make h probable," "h is probable in relation to e," and, "e confirms h." The properties of this relation are studied in detail in the logic of induction and the theory of mathematical probability. We consider here only certain of its very general features.[3]

To illustrate the logic of this relation, we consider the proposition:

(h)   John is a Democrat

and note the probability-relations that it bears to the following propositions:

(e)   26 of the 50 people in this room are Democrats, and John is in this room

(f)   26 of the 50 people who were in this room yesterday are not Democrats, and John was in this room yesterday

[2]James Van Cleve, "Epistemic Supervenience and the Circle of Belief," *The Monist*, Vol. 58 (1984), pp. 90–101; the quotation appears on page 100.

[3]The mathematical theory of probability investigates a somewhat more complex relation than the one considered here. One version of this more complex relation may be put as: "h is more probable than i in relation to e." The simpler relation with which we are here concerned may be defined in terms of the more complex relation as: "h is more probable than not-h in relation to e." This more complex relation is taken as primitive by Harold Jeffries, in *Theory of Probability* (Oxford: The Clarendon Press, 1939). Jeffries uses the expression: "Given p, q is more probable than r" (see p. 16).

(g)   45 of the 50 people who arrived on time are Democrats, and John arrived
            on time

(i)   99 of the 100 people who voted for the measure are not Democrats, and
            John voted for the measure

We may say that: (1) e tends to make h probable; (2) e&f does not tend to
make h probable; (3) e&f&g tends to make h probable; and (4) e&f&g&i
tends to make not-h probable.

What is intended by the locution, "e tends to make h probable," may be
put somewhat loosely by saying, "If *e* were the only relevant evidence you
had, then you would also have some justification for accepting *h*."

Our proposition e ("Most of the people in this room . . .") may not itself
be capable of being anyone's total evidence. But it is necessarily such that *if*
it is evident for a person S, then there is at least one proposition of the
following sort that is evident for S. The proposition will be one which is
such that it *could* be someone's total evidence, and it will necessarily be such
that anyone for whom it *is* the total evidence is someone for whom h is
probable.

We may define the relation of tending-to-make-probable this way:

D5   e tends to make h probable = Df   e is necessarily such that, for every x,
            if e is evident for x, then there is a w such that (i) w is evident for x, (ii) w&e
            is possibly such that it is someone's total evidence, and (iii) h is probable for
            anyone for whom w&e is the total evidence.

If a proposition e tends to make a proposition h probable, and if e&i does
not tend to make h probable, then the proposition i may be said to *defeat* the
confirmation that e tends to provide for h.[4] The relevant concept of defeat
is this:

D6   d defeats e's tendency to make h probable = Df   e tends to make h
            probable; and d&e does not tend to make h probable

APPLYING THE LOGICAL PROBABILITY RELATION

We now consider the *applied* probability relation expressed by, "e makes h
probable for S." The *logical* locution, "e tends to make h probable," as we
have said, expresses a relation that holds necessarily between propositions.

[4]The generic concept of defeat is discussed in detail in my "The Ethics of Requirement,"
American Philosophical Quarterly, Vol. I (1964), pp. 147–153. An improved and expanded
version is in "Practical Reason and the Logic of Requirement," in Stephan Körner, ed.,
Practical Reason (Oxford: Basil Blackwell, 1974), pp. 1–17; see also "Reply to Comments," pp.
40–53. Compare the discussion of defeat in John Pollock, *Knowledge and Justification* (Princeton, NJ: Princeton University Press, 1974), pp. 42–43; and Ernest Sosa, "The Foundations of
Foundationalism," *Nous*, Vol. 14 (1980), pp. 547–564; see especially p. 564.

But the *applied* locution expresses a contingent proposition: it applies the necessary relation to the beliefs of a particular person. The relation is this:

D6   e makes h probable for S = Df   (1) e is evident for S; (2) e tends to make
        h probable; (3) there is no d such that d is evident for S and d defeats e's
        tendency to make h probable; and (4) e does not entail h

Since the proposed definition contains the expression, "any proposition that is evident for S," the definition may be said to apply the *logical* probability relation to the *total evidence* of a particular subject.[5]

Our definition allows us to say that some but not all necessary propositions that are evident for S are such that something makes them probable for S. It also allows us to say that impossible propositions may be made probable for S. And this is as it should be. Each of us accepts some mathematical or logical propositions on authority; and the probability that such propositions have for us will be derived from certain contingent facts that we happen to know about the authorities in question.

In speaking of the application of probability, we must take care not to be mislead by writings about so-called "subjective probability." Some writers are interested in applying the probability relation to the *set of beliefs* that a person happens to have. But that application of the probability relation that is relevant to the theory of knowledge is the application to one's *total evidence*. It is not a matter of relating the hypothesis merely to *beliefs*. The set of propositions that a person accepts has members that are not *evident* for that person; and it may be that the set of propositions that are evident for that person may have members that he or she does not accept.

We noted in Chapter 2 that propositions that are merely probable for a subject S may yet be such that S is *more justified* in accepting some of them than in accepting others. In such cases we say that one of two merely probable propositions is "*more probable*" than the other for S. Whether we may assign numerical *degrees* to the probability that a proposition may have *for* a subject S is more problematic.[6]

---

[5]Bernard Bolzano seems to have been the first to be clear about this point. More recent philosophers who have stressed the concept of total evidence in applying the logical probability relation are John Maynard Keynes, Rudolf Carnap, and William Kneale. See Bernard Bolzano, *Theory of Science*, ed. Rolf George (Oxford: Basil Blackwell, 1972), p. 238, compare also pp. 238–245; 359–365. Bolzano's work was first published in 1837. Compare John Maynard Keynes, *A Treatise on Probability* (London: Macmillan and Co., Ltd. 1921), p. 4; Rudolf Carnap, *Logical Foundations of Probability* (Chicago, IL: University of Chicago Press, 1950), pp. 246–252; and William Kneale *Probability and Induction* (Oxford: The Clarendon Press, 1949), esp. pp. 9–13.

[6]I am indebted to Daniel Kervick and Paul McNamara for suggestions and criticisms. These questions are discussed in more detail in my article, "Probability in the Theory of Knowledge," in Marjorie Clay and Keith Lehrer, eds., *Theory of Knowledge: The State of the Art* (Dordrecht: D. Reidel, 1989).

AN ETHICAL ANALOGY

An ethical analogy may throw light upon the probability relation and its application.[7] Let us consider briefly the logic of *moral requirement*. Examples of moral requirement, as here understood, are: making a promise requires keeping the promise; wronging a person requires making up for the wrong; virtue (if Kant is right) requires being rewarded; and performing a sinful act requires punishment and repentance. The analogy between requirement and confirmation may be seen by constructing an example which parallels our illustration above of confirmation. For requirement may be defeated in just the ways in which confirmation may be defeated.

Consider the proposition:

(h)   The doctor should administer medical treatment to John

and note the requirement-relations that it bears to the following propositions:

(k)   John is seriously ill; and the doctor is in a position to try to treat him

(f)   John's wife is seriously ill; the doctor is in a position to try to treat her; but the doctor is in a position to treat only one of them

(g)   The doctor is himself seriously ill and his treating John would aggravate John's illness

(i)   If the doctor were to treat John, the treatment would temporarily aggravate John's illness but would subsequently cure the illness; and the illness of Johns' wife cannot be treated or relieved

We may say that: (1) k requires h; (2) k&f does not require h; (3) k&f&g requires not-h; and (4) k&f&g&i requires h.

The relevant concept of *defeat* is this:

D7   s defeats p's requirement for q = Df   (i) p requires q, (ii) p&s does not require q, and (iii) p&s is logically compatible with q

The example enables us to understand W. D. Ross's distinction between *prima facie* duties (something requires *one to act in a* certain way) and absolute duties (one *ought* to act in a certain way).[8] And thus they enable us to say in what sense there *can* be said to be a conflict of duties (there can be conflicts of *prima facie* duties) and in what sense there can *not* be said to be a conflict of duties (there cannot be conflicts of absolute duties).

[7]I have discussed this analogy in detail in "Epistemic Reasoning and the Logic of Epistemic Concepts," in G. H. von Wright, ed., *Logic and Philosophy* (The Hague: Martinus Nijhoff, 1980), pp. 71–78.

[8]See W. D. Ross, *The Right and the Good* (Oxford: The Clarendon Press, 1930), p. 18.

Thus we could say:

D8   S has an absolute duty to perform A = Df   There occurs an x such that
          x requires S to perform A, and there occurs no y such that y defeats x's
          requirement that S perform A

This absolute sense of duty is analogous, then, to the absolute sense of the
probability relation.[9]

There is a fundamental analogy, then, between the logic of moral
requirement and that of confirmation. In setting forth the principles of
moral requirement, we have used *"prima facie* duty" and have contrasted
prima facie duties with what Ross called *"absolute* duties." In setting forth the
principles of confirmation, we could have used an analogous terminology,
contrasting *"prima facie* probability" with what, following Bolzano, we could
call *"absolute* probability." For we may say that, if e tends to make h probable and if e is evident for S, then there is a *prima facie* case for saying that h
is probable for S. And we could say that, if e *makes* h probable *for* S, then h is
absolutely probable for S. These uses of *"prima facie"* and *"absolutely"* may be
extended to other epistemic terms. According to Meinong and Price, as we
have seen, if e tends to make h evident and if e is evident for S, then there is
a *prima facie* case for saying that h is evident for S. The concepts of *prima
facie* probability and *prima facie* evidence, as we shall see, are essential to
understanding certain contemporary issues in theory of knowledge.

THE RELATION OF EPISTEMIC JUSTIFICATION TO MORAL DUTY

We are now in a position to consider one of the fundamental questions
about the nature of epistemic justification. What is the relation between the
justification of belief and moral duty?

Those who feel that there is *no* real connection between duty and the
justification of belief emphasize that our believings and withholdings are
not actions in the ordinary sense of the word. They may reason, "You can
order a person to perform certain types of action. But surely there is no
point in ordering a person to *believe* any proposition. Even if I desperately
wanted to believe, say, that the Vietnamese war had never taken place, I
don't have the strength of will that would be required to make myself
believe it—at least to make myself believe it *now*. Therefore, if you speak of

---

[9]There are other ethical situations that throw light upon the concept of defeat. Within the
theory of intrinsic value, we may say of certain states of affairs, not only that they are, say,
good, but also that they are *indefeasibly good*—where an indefeasibly good state of affairs is a
good state of affairs which is such that there is *no* state of affairs that would defeat its
goodness. We have left open here the question whether this concept is applicable in epistemology. I have discussed indefeasible good and evil in *Brentano and Intrinsic Value*
(Cambridge, England: Cambridge University Press, 1986), Chapter VIII.

moral duty and the justification of belief in the same breath, you are confusing two entirely different categories. And this means that you are misconstruing the whole point of traditional theory of knowledge." There are a number of points that may be made in reply. For present purposes, it is enough to emphasize only one.[10]

We have seen that a single normative locution will suffice to characterize the various levels and types of epistemic concept. We have put the locution as, "A is more justified than B for S," where the letters "A" and "B" refer to doxastic states—to believings and withholdings. This epistemic locution may be construed as expressing a *requirement to prefer*. And this fact provides us with the answer to the above objection.

To be required to *prefer* something A to something B is to be required not to choose between A and B without choosing A. Hence the requirement is a negative one: the person is required *not* to choose between A and B without thereby choosing A. Like most negative requirements, the requirement-to-prefer can ordinarily be fulfilled without any great effort of will. Presumably you are now fulfilling quite effortlessly the requirement not to steal your neighbor's dog. And in a similar way you may be fulfilling the requirement not to prefer withholding the proposition that there are no round squares to believing that proposition.

Epistemic requirement is only one type of requirement. There are also the requirements of *etiquette*, or *good manners*—what Thomas Hobbes called "Small Moralls." And there are *aesthetic* requirements. If the host is discoursing, perhaps the social situation requires that you not interrupt him. But this requirement is defeated, or overridden, if you see that the house is on fire. And if the painter puts colors of one sort here, then aesthetic considerations may require that he put colors of another sort there. But these requirements are overridden if he is hastily painting an exit sign so that the guests can escape. Epistemic requirements, analogously, may be overridden by non-epistemic considerations.

Consider a person who has been brought into the emergency ward. He has the duty to make himself well enough to fulfill certain obligations, and he knows that he will do so only if he believes in the competence of the attending physician. But such evidence that he has points to the incompetence of the physician. In such a case, the patient may be *morally* required to prefer believing that his physician is competent to believing that he is not competent.

What, then, is the distinctive feature of an epistemic requirement?

A consequence of our "internalistic" theory of knowledge is that, if one is subject to an epistemic requirement at any time, then this requirement is

---

[10]The resemblances between believings and withholdings, on the one hand, and other types of actions, on the other, are discussed in: C. I. Lewis, *The Ground and Nature of the Right* (New York: Columbia University Press, 1955), Chapter 2, "Right Believing and Concluding" (pp. 20–38); and C. S. Peirce, *Collected Papers*, Volume I (Cambridge, MA: Harvard University Press, 1931), paragraph 1.607.

imposed by the *conscious state* in which one happens to find oneself at that time. But the distinction between epistemic and other types of requirement does *not* lie in the fact that only the former is imposed by one's conscious state. For our beliefs, which are a part of our conscious state, may also impose *moral* requirements.

An epistemic requirement, unlike an ethical requirement, may be imposed by a part of one's conscious state that includes no belief that imposes that requirement. For example, it is beyond reasonable doubt for me that the person I now see walking is the same as the person I saw walking a moment ago. This means that I am required to prefer accepting that proposition to withholding it. And the requirement is imposed by a part of my conscious state that contains *no* beliefs that have a content that imposes that requirement. This, then, is the distinguishing feature of epistemic requirement and therefore the distinguishing feature of epistemic justification.

The distinguishing feature of moral duty is that it is a requirement that is not defeated by any other requirement. An epistemic requirement, therefore, may become a moral duty.[11]

---

[11]These questions are discussed in detail by Roderick Firth in: "Chisholm and the Ethics of Belief," *Philosophical Review*, Vol. LXVIII (1959), pp. 493–506; "Are Epistemic Concepts Reducible to Ethical Concepts," in Alvin Goldman and Jaegwon Kim, eds., *Values and Morals* (Dordrecht: D. Reidel, 1978), pp. 215–230; and "Epistemic Merit, Intrinsic and Instrumental," *Proceedings and Addresses of the American Philosophical Association*, Vol. LIII (1981), pp. 5–23.

CHAPTER 7

The Structure of Empirical Knowledge

INTRODUCTION

We now sketch *one* general theory about the structure of our empirical knowledge. The theory is *internalistic* and, as we shall see later, it may also be called *foundational*. In the following chapter, we will consider whether there is any serious alternative to an internalistic epistemology. And in the chapter after that, we will consider whether there is any serious alternative to a foundational epistemology.

We will set forth certain *criteria* for the application of our epistemic concepts—such concepts as being certain, being evident, and being probable. These concepts, as we have said, are *normative*: they imply something about epistemic *justification*. A criterion for the application of any such concept will formulate certain conditions under which the normative concept may be applied.

Following one tradition in moral philosophy, we will call our criteria *material* epistemic principles and contrast them with *formal* epistemic principles.

A *formal* epistemic principle is a principle relating one epistemic concept to another. Examples are, "Whatever is evident is beyond reasonable doubt," and, "If anything is probable, then something is certain." A *material* epistemic principle is a principle relating non-epistemic concepts to epistemic concepts. An example is, "If a person believes himself to be talking with someone, then it is certain for that person that he believes himself to be talking with someone." The antecedent of the principle tells us that the applicability of a certain non-normative concept (believing oneself to be talking with someone) constitutes a sufficient logical condition for the application of a certain normative concept (being certain that one believes oneself to be talking with someone).

The ten material epistemic principles that we will formulate here will be somewhat more general. They will be "internal" in that the proper use of them at any time will enable us to ascertain the epistemic status of our own beliefs at that time. Our first principle, which we discussed in Chapter 3, will be a criterion for what is *certain*; application of this principle is presupposed by our other principles. Then we will mark off, in order, that which is epistemically *probable*, that which is *in the clear*, that which is *beyond reasonable doubt*, and that which is *evident*.

By means of such principles we can show just how it is that a proposition may acquire positive epistemic status for a subject S. And we can show this without calling upon other justified propositions whose justification remains unaccounted for. Most alternative accounts of the structure of empirical knowledge do not succeed in doing this.

At the end of the chapter, we will consider the epistemic status of these principles themselves.

THE FIRST STEP: THE CERTAIN

In pursuing traditional epistemology, we begin by sorting out those of our beliefs that are *certain*. We begin here since the application of each of our material epistemic principles requires that we appeal to something that is certain. It is mainly because of this fact that the present view may be called "foundational."

In Chapter 3, we introduced the following concept of a self-presenting property:

D1   P is self-presenting = Df   Every property that P entails includes the
        property of thinking

Then we formulated the first of our material principles:

MP1   If the property of being F is self-presenting, if S is F, and if S believes
         himself to be F, then it is certain for S that he is F

We thus use the letter "S" to refer to any believing person. Since our inquiry is a Socratic one, we may think of "S" in the first instance as designating ourselves. But our principles are intended to be general principles that are applicable to *all* believing subjects.

THE SECOND STEP: THE PROBABLE

We next formulate two principles about the application of probability.

We assume first that having a given belief tends to make the object of that belief probable. In other words:

MP2   Accepting h tends to make h probable

This is *not* to say that a proposition is made probable *for* you by the mere fact that you accept it. That would be what Richard Foley has called "epistemic conservatism."[1] And it would hardly be reasonable. For it would imply that, no matter how much evidence you have for a given proposition, you could make the negation of that proposition probable for you merely by accepting that negation.

What we are affirming is, not that accepting a proposition *makes* that proposition probable for the one who accepts it, but rather that accepting a proposition *tends* to make that proposition probable—in the sense of "tending-to-make-probable" that we defined in the previous chapter. Our principle could be said to express "epistemic *commonsensism*" rather than "epistemic conservatism." An alternative terminology may make the distinction more clear.

We have noted how the expression "*prima facie* probable" might be used and contrasted with what Bolzano had called the "*absolute*" sense of probability. If e tends to make h probable and if e is evident for S, then there is a *prima facie* case for saying that h is probable for S. The expression "*prima facie* probable" has been used to describe this situation. And if e *makes* h probable *for* S, then h is *absolutely* probable for S. Using these expressions, we may now describe the distinction between epistemic conservatism and epistemic commonsensism. Epistemic conservatism tells us that accepting a proposition makes that proposition *absolutely* probable for the person who accepts it. Epistemic commonsensism, on the other hand, tells us only that accepting a proposition makes that proposition *prima facie* probable for the person who accepts it.

How, then, are we to *apply* this principle? We add the following:

MP3   If S accepts h and if h is not disconfirmed by S's total evidence, then h is
         probable for S

(To say that "h is disconfirmed by e" is to say that e tends to make not-h

---

[1]See Richard Foley,"Epistemic Conservatism," *Philosophical Studies*, Vol. 43 (1983), pp. 165–182. Foley observes, correctly, that in earlier writings I have been guilty of epistemic conservatism. This has also been pointed out by Richard Fumerton in *Metaphysical and Epistemological Problems of Perception* (Lincoln: University of Nebraska Press, 1985), p. 27ff.

probable.) This principle allows us to use Peirce's term and describe our commonsensism as *"critical* commonsensism."[2]

Believing that God exists, then, could make it probable for you that God does exist. So, too, for believing that God does not exist. What, then, is the epistemic difference between the belief that God exists and the belief that the devil is persecuting you? If the natural theologian can do his work, then the former belief may be better able to survive critical scrutiny and become *probable* for those who know this work.[3] But we shall not look into this question here.

THE THIRD STEP: THAT WHICH IS IN THE CLEAR

We now have a set of propositions that are *probable* for S; these comprise those propositions that are accepted by S and are not disconfirmed by his total evidence. We may now go on to single out a subset of these probable propositions. The subset will comprise those probable propositions that are not disconfirmed by the whole set of propositions that are probable for S. Our third material principle tells us that such propositions are epistemically in the clear for S: S is at least as justified in accepting any such proposition as he is in withholding it.

MP4   If S accepts h and if not-h is not probable in relation to the set of propositions that are probable for S, then h is epistemically in the clear for S

Hence the content of a common sense belief acquires higher epistemic status by being one of those common sense beliefs that is not disconfirmed by one's total evidence.

THE FOURTH STEP: THAT WHICH IS BEYOND REASONABLE DOUBT

We will now try to ascend from that which is epistemically in the clear for S to that which is beyond reasonable doubt for S. To do so, we will consider perception once again.

In discussing the evidence of the senses, we concluded that some version

[2]See Charles Sanders Peirce, *Collected Papers*, Vol. V (Cambridge, MA: Harvard University Press, 1934), pp. 346–375 (paragraphs 497–533).

[3]For a recent attempt to develop a natural theology, see Richard Swinburne, *The Existence of God* (Oxford: The Clarendon Press, 1979). Swinburne concludes that "on our total evidence theism is more probable than not" (p. 291). Recent studies on the relevance of recent studies in epistemology to Christian theology may be found in Alvin Plantinga and Nicholas Wolterstorff, eds., *Faith and Rationality: Reason and Belief in God* (Notre Dame: Notre Dame University Press, 1983); this work includes papers by Plantinga, Woltersdorf, William Alston, George Mavrodes, George Marsden, and David Holwerda.

of the "critical" theory of Carneades is the only alternative to skepticism. Speaking somewhat loosely, we may put the theory this way: if a proposition that is epistemically in the clear is an object of a perceptual taking (an object of what is thought to be a perception), then the proposition is *beyond reasonable doubt*, that is, one is more justified in believing it than in withholding it. If you think that you see familiar pieces of furniture in front of you, then the fact that you *do* think that you see those things lends respectability to your belief about what you see.

To formulate our perceptual principle, let us recall our definitions of what we have called "perceptual taking" and of perceiving:

D2   S takes there to be an F = Df S is appeared — to; it is evident to S that he is appeared — to; and S believes that there is only one thing that is appearing — to him and that that thing is F

D3   S perceives that there is an F = Df (1) There is an F that is appearing in a certain way to S; (2) S takes there to be an F that is appearing to him in that way; and (3) it is evident to S that an F is appearing to him in that way

We now affirm the following principle about *perceptual taking*:

MP5   If S *takes* there to be an F, and if it is epistemically in the clear for him that there is an F which he takes to be F, then it is *beyond reasonable doubt* for S that he is perceiving something to be F

Applying this principle, then, we arrive at a set of propositions that are beyond reasonable doubt.

Why not make the principle simpler and omit the second part of the antecedent ("if it is epistemically in the clear for him that there is an F which he takes to be F")? The simpler version of the principle was proposed in the first edition of this book. That some qualification is necessary, however, was pointed out by Herbert Heidelberger. He observed that, in its unqualified form, the principle

tells us that if a man believes that he perceives a certain object to be yellow then the proposition that he does perceive that object to be yellow and the proposition that that object is yellow are reasonable for him. But let us suppose that the following facts are known by that man: there is a yellow light shining on the object, he remembers having perceived a moment ago that the object was white, and at that time there was no colored light shining on the object. Suppose that, in spite of this evidence, he believes that he perceives that the object is yellow. It would not be correct to say that for our man the proposition that the object is yellow is a reasonable one. Merely from the fact that a man believes that he perceives something to have a certain property *F*, it does not follow, accordingly, that the proposition that that something is *F* is a reasonable one for him; for, as in our example, he may have other evidence which, when combined with the evidence that he believes that he perceives something to have *F*, may make the proposition that something is *F* highly unreasonable.[4]

[4]Herbert Heidelberger, in "Chisholm's Epistemic Principles," *Nous*, III (1969), pp. 73–82; the quotation is on p. 75.

Let us consider two further examples.

Suppose a person believes that he perceives a sheep in the field: he *takes* there to be a sheep in the field before him. Suppose further that he *also* has good reason to believe that his senses are deceiving him. Perhaps he has been told that he will be deceived. Or perhaps he knows that others, in the type of situation in which he happens to find himself, were deluded; they too, thought they saw a sheep—but no sheep was there to be seen. In such a case, the proposition that he does perceive a sheep might *not* be one that is beyond reasonable doubt for him.

A slightly different example is provided by the case of "the authoritative epistemologist." His impressionable student *takes* something to be a sheep. But the epistemologist has set forth certain arguments designed to show that one should not trust the senses, and by the force of his personality he has persuaded the student that the arguments are sound. The result is that, for the student, it is no longer epistemically in the clear that there *is* a sheep that he takes to be a sheep. Hence we need not say that it is beyond reasonable doubt for him that he is perceiving something to be a sheep.

And so we do not say that the object of a perceptual taking is, as such, beyond reasonable doubt. We say that, *if* the object is epistemically in the clear, *then* it is beyond reasonable doubt. And this is what Carneades had said, "The wise man will make use of whatever apparently probable presentation he encounters, if nothing presents itself that is contrary to that probability."[5]

What if one takes something to be a sheep but does so "solely because of wishful thinking?"[6] We should note, first, that one cannot take something to be a sheep *solely* because of wishful thinking. Moreover, according to the internalistic theory of justification that is presupposed here, epistemic *justification* is not a function of the *causes* of one's belief. (This matter will be discussed in detail in the following chapter.)

THE ROLE OF APPEARING

We have, then, certain principles telling us how facts about *appearances* may justify us in certain beliefs about the *external things* that present those appearances. These principles, it is important to note, do not presuppose that appearances somehow "mirror" or "copy" the things of which they *are* the appearances. They do not tell us that we *read off* the nature of things

[5]Cicero, op. cit., p. 595.

[6]See the discussion of this question in Paul K. Moser, *Empirical Justification* (Dordrecht: D. Reidel, 1985), Chapter V.

from the nature of their appearances.[7] The ground for our material principles does not lie in any presuppositions about resemblance. And therefore the present view is not subject to one criticism that is often made of foundational theories.

It could be that there are extra-terrestrial beings who aren't appeared to at all. What kind of justification would *they* have for their beliefs about the external things around them?[8] If such beings are not appeared to at all, then it is not clear that they *have* any justification for such beliefs. This is not to say, however, that man is the measure of all things. There may well be other beings who are appeared to in ways that we cannot even imagine and who know even more about the external world than we do. But if they *are* appeared to, if their sensings depend upon external physical stimuli in the way that ours do, then all that is needed is that they *take* certain sensible properties to be ways of being appeared to and that these takings be related, in some such way as that described here, to other self-presenting properties.

Our principle implies that it is reasonable to interpret ways of being appeared to as being reports from the outside. One may ask, then, how the role of appearances differs from that of mere hunches that one might have about external things.[9] One might have a strong feeling, for example, that a bolt of lightning is on the way. Couldn't this feeling also be taken to be a report from the outside? And if this is so, how do such feelings or hunches differ from ways of being appeared to?

In the case of being appeared to, there *is* something, one's being appeared to in a certain way, that one interprets as being a *sign* of some external fact. But just *having* the hunch that lightning is on the way is not, in the same sense, to interpret something as being a sign from the outside.

What if one has a belief *about* one's hunch and interprets *it* as being a sign of lightning about to come? This, of course, is not quite like the case where we interpret an appearance as being the appearance *of* an external thing. But if one were to interpret the hunch as being a kind of external prodding and were to assume that it is a way of being prodded *by* an external bolt of

---

[7]See the criticism of such "mirror" theories in Richard Rorty, *Philosophy and the Mirror of Nature* (Princeton, NJ: Princeton University Press, 1979), pp. 70–78. Compare Ernest Sosa's discussion of the "foundationalist's dilemma," in "The Raft and the Pyramid," *Midwestern Studies in Philosophy*, Vol. V (1980), pp. 3–25, esp. pp. 20–23. Sosa is concerned with those foundationalists who argue that under certain circumstances we can know that external things are red by knowing that they present appearances that are red. Such foundationalists have not realized that "red" occurs ambiguously in such statements as, "The appearance is red and the external thing is red." As we have seen, the sense in which an *appearance* may be said to be red is quite different from that in which an *external physical thing* may be said to be red.

[8]Sosa raises this question; op. cit., p. 22.

[9]This question is suggested by Ernest Sosa in "The Raft and the Pyramid," *Midwest Studies in Philosophy*, Vol. V (1980), pp. 3–25; see pp. 20–23.

lightning, then, perhaps, we would have to say of "being prodded by" pretty much what we have said about "being appeared to by."

REMEMBERING

By reference to perceptual taking, we have singled out a set of propositions that are beyond reasonable doubt for S. We may now increase the members of this set by reference to remembering.

The word "memory" presents us with terminological problems analogous to those presented by the word "perception." We have noted that, if "perception" is taken in its ordinary sense, then "unveridical perception" is a contradictory expression. We must distinguish what we *perceive* a thing to be from what we *take* it to be—or *think* we perceive it to be. Discussing the problem of memory, Cicero noted a similar situation and asked, "How can there possibly be a memory that is false?"[10]

Consider a situation in which, as one might say, a person's memory has "deceived him": the person would have said, honestly and sincerely, that he remembered a certain event to have occurred but, actually, the event did not occur at all. Such deceptions of memory are common; "we remember remembering things and later finding them to be false."[11] But if we say, "What he remembered is false," the ordinary interpretation of the word "remember" will render what we say contradictory; hence, if we wish to restrict "remember" to its ordinary use, we must express the fact in question by saying, "What he *seemed* to remember is false." And of those cases where one's memory is not thus deceptive, we should say, "What he seemed to remember is true."

Our principle about memory, then, is analogous to that about perception:

MP6   If S *seems to remember* having been F, and if it is epistemically in the clear for him that he remembers having been F, then it is *beyond reasonable doubt* for S that he remembers having been F

An analogous principle about memory has been set forth by other philosophers—for example, by A. Meinong, Bertrand Russell, and C. I. Lewis.[12]

[10]Op. cit., p. 497.

[11]C. I. Lewis, *An Analysis of Knowledge and Valuation* (La Salle, Ill.: Open Court Publishing Co., 1946), p. 334.

[12]See A. Meinong, "Toward an Epistemological Assessment of Memory," in Roderick M. Chisholm and Robert Swartz, eds., *Empirical Knowledge* (Englewood Cliffs, NJ: Prentice-Hall, Inc., 1973), pp. 253–270; Bertrand Russell, *An Inquiry into Meaning and Truth* (New York: W. W. Norton and Co., Inc., 1940), pp. 192–202; and C. I. Lewis, *An Analysis of Knowledge and Valuation* (La Salle, IL: The Open Court Publishing Company, 1946), Ch. XI.

Since both memory and perception are capable of playing us false, we run a twofold risk when we appeal to the memory of a perception. Suppose a person thinks he remembers having seen a cat on the roof. The situation presents us with four possibilities.

(1) the present memory and the past perception are both veridical: he did think he perceived a cat and what he saw was, in fact, a cat.

(2) He correctly remembers having thought he saw a cat, but what he saw was not a cat. In this second case, the fault lies with the past perception and not with the present memory.

(3) He incorrectly remembers having thought he saw a cat; but what he really thought he saw, at the time, was a squirrel, and in fact it *was* a squirrel that he saw. In this case, the fault lies with the present memory and not with the past perception.

(4) He thinks he remembers having thought he saw a cat; but what he thought he saw, at the time, was a squirrel, and the perception was unveridical for there was no squirrel there at all. In this fourth case, the fault lies both with the present memory and the past perception. As we know, however, memory, by a kind of happy failure, if not an act of dishonesty, may correct the past perception. The person thought he saw a squirrel, but it was in fact a cat, and now he thinks he remembers that he thought he saw a cat. Ordinary language provides us with no clear way of distinguishing these different types of deception, and memory may receive more blame than it deserves.[13] But it would seem that the deliverances of memory should receive a lower degree of credence than those of perception.

CONCURRENCE

Sometimes propositions *mutually support* each other. When this happens, each of the mutually supporting propositions may be said to add to the positive epistemic status of the other. This concept of mutual support, or *concurrence*, goes back to the Greek skeptic Carneades. In illustrating Carneades' view, Sextus Empiricus cites a group of perceptions all concurring in the fact that a certain man is Socrates. "We believe that this man is Socrates from the fact that he possesses all his customary qualities—colour, size, shape, converse, coat, and his position in a place where there is no one like him." Concurrence is also illustrated in medical diagnoses: "Some doctors do not deduce that it is a true case of fever from one symptom only—such as too quick a pulse or a very high temperature—but from a con-

---

[13]Compare Andrew Naylor, "Remembering without Knowing," *Philosophical Studies*, Vol. 49 (1986), pp. 295–312.

currence, such as that of a high temperature with a rapid pulse and ulcerous joints and flushing and thirst and analogous symptoms."[14]

When Carneades said that certain sets of propositions are concurrent, he meant that each member of such a set would support, and also be supported by, the other members of the set. We could say that any set of propositions that are mutually consistent and logically independent of each other is concurrent provided that each member of the set is probable in relation to the conjunction of all the members of the set.[15]

We will now describe mutual support more precisely.

Two propositions that entail each other and are thus doxastically equivalent may be said to stand in a relation of mutual support. But what of propositions that do not even imply each other? Can we find a proposition h and a proposition e which are such that neither implies the other and each is probable in relation to the other? This does not appear to be possible. That is to say, we cannot find *two* empirical propositions, e and h, which are such that (i) e is probable in relation to h and (ii) h is probable in relation to e. But it is not difficult to find three propositions, e, h, and i, which are such that: (i) e is probable in relation to h and i, (ii) h is probable in relation to e and i, and (iii) i is probable in relation to e and h.

An example would be:

(e)   Most of the people here are friendly; and John is here if and only if Mary is here

(h)   John is here and is friendly

(i)   Mary is here and is friendly

The conjunction of any two of these propositions is such that it *tends* to make the third probable. But no *one* of these propositions tends to make either of the others probable. We may say that such propositions mutually support each other.

---

[14]*Sextus Empiricus*, Vol. II, para. 178–179, p. 97. Sextus also cites this example: "When a rope is lying coiled up in a dark room, to one who enters hurriedly it presents the simply 'probable' appearance of being a serpent; but to the man who has looked carefully round and has investigated the conditions—such as its immobility and its colour, and each of its other peculiarities—it appears as a rope in accordance with an impression that is probable and tested." Vol. I, p. 141.

[15]Compare the definition of "coherence" in H. H. Price's *Perception*, p. 183, and the definition of "congruence" in C. I. Lewis' *An Analysis of Knowledge and Valuation*, p. 338; Lewis discusses the logical properties of this concept in detail. See also Roderick Firth, "Coherence, Certainty, and Epistemic Priority," *Journal of Philosophy*, Vol. LXI (1964), pp. 545–557; Nicholas Rescher, *The Coherence Theory of Truth* (London: Oxford University Press, 1973), 53–71; Keith Lehrer, *Knowledge* (London: Oxford University Press), pp. 154–186; Richard Foley, "Chisholm and Coherence," *Philosophical Studies*, Vol. 38 (1980), pp. 53–63; Noah M. Lemos, "Coherence and Epistemic Priority," *Philosophical Studies*, Vol. 41 (1982), pp. 299–315; and Laurence Bonjour, *The Structure of Empirical Knowledge* (Cambridge, MA: Harvard University Press, 1985), pp. 87ff.

Carneades had spoken of concurring presentations as hanging together like "links in a chain." But Meinong's figure may be more illuminating, "One may think of playing-cards. No one of them is capable of standing by itself, but several of them, leaned against other, can serve to hold each other up."[16] Each of the propositions in our concurrent set must be acceptable on its own if we are to derive reasonability from concurrence, just as each of the members of a house of cards must have its own degree of substance and rigidity if the house is not to collapse. (We may be reluctant to compare reasonability with a house of cards. In this event, Meinong has another figure for us: a stack of weapons in the field, each leaning toward the center and thus helping to hold up all the others.)

The relevant sense of "mutual support" is this:

D4   A is a set of propositions that are *concurrent* for S DF   A is a set of three or more propositions each of which is made probable for S by the conjunction of the others

Our principle about perceptual taking (MP5) yielded a set of perceptual propositions that are beyond reasonable doubt. By appealing to the fact of concurrence, we are now able to specify certain other propositions that are beyond reasonable doubt. For we may formulate a principle enabling us to ascend from a set of propositions that are epistemically in the clear to a set of propositions that are beyond reasonable doubt:

MP7   If there is a set of concurrent propositions such that all of the propositions are epistemically in the clear for S and one of them is beyond reasonable doubt for S, then all of them are beyond reasonable doubt for S

Concurrence, then, plays an important role in the present account of the structure of empirical knowledge.

THE FIFTH STEP: THE EVIDENT

And now we are able to ascend to what is *evident*:

MP8   If *being appeared — to* is evident for S, and if it is epistemically in the clear for S that there is something that appears — to him, then it is *evident* for S that there is something that is appearing — to him

Application of this principle yields an *evident* belief that goes beyond what is

---

[16]A. Meinong, *Über Möglichkeit und Wahrscheinlichkeit* (1915), p. 465; this work now constitutes Volume VI of *Alexius Meinong Gesamtausgabe* (Graz: Akademisches Druck- und Verlagsanstalt, 1972), edited by Rudolf Haller and Rudolf Kindinger.

self-presenting. This principle tells us of conditions under which *being appeared to* makes it evident that *something* is appearing.

Our principle MP5 described conditions under which it is beyond reasonable doubt for S that he is perceiving something to be F. Now we are able to ascend further in the epistemic scale and describe conditions under which it is *evident* for S that he perceives something to be F:

MP9   If S takes there to be an F and if it is beyond reasonable doubt for S that he is perceiving something to be F, then it is *evident* for S that he is perceiving something to be F

We have been able to single out, then, a type of proposition that is evident and that goes beyond what is self-presenting and what is *a priori*.

Our concurrence principle MP7 above yielded a class of propositions all of which are beyond reasonable doubt. Applying now our new perceptual principle MP9 to this concurrent set, we are able to attain still other propositions that are evident. We may say that, if any member of such a set is evident, then the other members of that set are also evident:

MP10   If there is a set of concurrent propositions such that all of them are beyond reasonable doubt for S and one of them is evident for S, then all of them are evident for S

THE JUSTIFICATION OF EPISTEMIC PRINCIPLES

We have formulated two types of material epistemic principle. (1) Those of the first type are *prima facie*, or *unapplied*, epistemic principles: they do not refer to a particular subject, but merely relate propositions, telling us what it is that certain propositions *tend* to justify. (2) Principles of the second type are *applied* material principles, telling us how principles of the first type may be applied to the total evidence of any particular subject.

The *prima facie*, or *unapplied*, principles include the following:

MP2   Accepting h tends to make h probable

The applied principles include the following:

MP4   Is S accepts h and if h is not disconfirmed by S's total evidence, then h is probable for S

What may we say about the *justification* for such principles?

It would not be plausible to say that they are *a priori* since many philosophers have understood them without thereby seeing that they are true.

We will have a better conception of the status of these principles if we consider them in connection with that general presupposition which, as we have said, the epistemologist makes when he asks his Socratic questions:

I am justified in believing that I can improve and correct my system of beliefs. Of those beliefs that are about matters of interest or concern to me, I can eliminate the ones that are unjustified and add others that are justified; and I can replace less justified beliefs about those topics by beliefs that are more justified.

Consider now those conditional propositions that are formed by using this presupposition as antecedent and using any of our epistemic principles, applied or unapplied, as consequent. I suggest that these conditional propositions *can* be known *priori* to be true. This means that, for any subject S, for whom any such conditional is evident, the consequent of that conditional is at least as justified as is the antecedent. If this is true, then our material principles, applied and unapplied, are at least as justified for us as is that faith in oneself with which the epistemologist sets out.

No one can give us a reason for *not* accepting this much. One might hope for more. But this *epistemic predicament*, as we may call it, is essential to our subject; there is no more satisfactory method available. When one investigates the questions of the theory of knowledge, the *first* move that one makes—the first assumption that one makes or acts upon—can *only* be of this sort. And this is true no matter what the theory may be that one hopes to be able to defend.

Some will feel that the material principles we have set forth here are too permissive. And others will feel that they are not permissive enough. The skeptic, if he allowed himself to discuss the matter, would say we should not countenance the possibility that some of our beliefs are justified. The "immediatist"—the one who concedes that certain facts are self-presenting but who refuses to go beyond these facts—will say that we go too far in permitting any trust in what we call perception and memory. The proponent of "*Verstehen*" will say that we have not gone far enough. He or she thinks that our intuitive understanding of the thoughts and feelings of other people justifies us in certain beliefs about such thoughts and feelings.[17] The religious intuitionist adds that certain other thoughts and feelings justify us in believing that there is a personal God. Some go still further, saying, in effect, "I have certain thoughts and feelings that justify me in believing, not only that there is a personal God, but also that this God has selected *me*, out of all others, to be his personal representative."

Those of us who take a stand on these epistemological questions and who do not find ourselves at either of the two extremes may expect to be criticized by philosophers who do not go as far as we do and also by philosophers who go even farther. We may find that it is difficult to respond to

---

[17]Some of the issues that are involved are discussed in my book, *The Foundations of Knowing* (Brighton and Minneapolis: Harvesters Limited and the University of Minnesota Press, 1982), pp. 86–94. See also: Wilhelm Dilthey, *Gesammelte Schriften*, Vol. 5 (Leipzig and Berlin: B. G. Teubner, 1924), pp. 317–38; Max Scheler, *The Nature of Sympathy* (London: Routledge & Kegan Paul, 1964); and Alfred Schuetz, "Scheler's Theory of Intersubjectivity and the General Thesis of the Alter Ego." *Philosophy and Phenomenological Research*, Vol. 3 (1942), pp. 323–45.

the one without thereby giving in to the other. This fact, too, is a consequence of the epistemic predicament—a predicament which most writers on the theory of knowledge prefer not to recognize.

CONCLUSION

Here, then, is one way of completing the task of the traditional epistemologist. The system here set forth is not a version of skepticism or of subjectivism. It implies that what is *evident* for us may include propositions about the external things we perceive and propositions about what we remember. The principles that we have set forth do not take us beyond this point. Our "commonsensism," therefore, is not only critical but also moderate.

In the two chapters that follow we will ask whether there are actual alternatives to the present approach to our subject. We will find that, at best, the proposed alternatives are somewhat more programatic than what has been set forth here.

CHAPTER 8

Internalism and Externalism

"All knowledge is knowledge of someone; and ultimately no one can have any ground for his beliefs which does not lie within his own experience." C. I. Lewis[1]

INTRODUCTION

We now turn to the dispute between those who would interpret epistemic justification "internally" and those who would interpret it "externally."[2] The dispute concerns the proper analysis of the concept of epistemic justification; it presupposes, therefore, that the internalists and externalists share a common concept of justification—the one that distinguishes knowledge from true belief that is not knowledge.

We must be on guard, however, in interpreting contemporary literature that professes to be about "internalism" or "externalism." Some of those authors who profess to view knowledge and epistemic justification "externally" are not concerned with traditional theory of knowledge. That is to say, they are not concerned with the Socratic questions, "What can I know?" "How can I be sure that my beliefs are justified?" and "How can I

---

[1]*An Analysis of Knowledge and Valuation* (La Salle: The Open Court Publishing Company, 1946), p. 236.

[2]For early statements of the distinction, see "The Internalist Conception of Justification," by Alvin Goldman, in *Midwestern Studies in Philosophy*, Vol. V (1980), pp. 27–51, and "Externalist Conceptions of Empirical Knowledge," by Laurence Bonjour, *ibid*, pp. 53–74.

improve my present stock of beliefs?" Indeed many such philosophers are not concerned with the analysis of any ordinary concept of knowledge or of epistemic justification. Therefore their enterprise, whatever it may be, is not that of traditional theory of knowledge. My concern in what follows pertains only to the epistemological dispute, Is the concept of epistemic justification to be analysed internally or externally?

I will begin by saying what I understand by "internalism."

WHAT IS "INTERNALISM"?

The usual approach to the traditional questions of theory of knowledge is properly called "internal" or "internalistic." The internalist assumes that, merely by reflecting upon his own conscious state, he can formulate a set of epistemic principles that will enable him to find out, with respect to any possible belief he has, whether he is *justified* in having that belief. The epistemic principles that he formulates are principles that one may come upon and apply merely by sitting in one's armchair, so to speak, and without calling for any outside assistance. In a word, one need consider only one's own state of mind. But if we look at the matter, it seems clear that the approach to the questions of the traditional theory of knowledge can only be thus internalistic.

To be sure, we can assess the beliefs that *other* people have without examining *their* states of mind. And we can assess the beliefs that we ourselves have had at *other times* without examining the states of mind that *we* had at those other times. But these assessments although "external" in one sense, are "internal" in another.

Suppose we are considering the beliefs that some other persons had yesterday. After the fact, we may have information enabling us to assess their beliefs and to note just where they made their mistakes and where they did not. The principles we use need not be principles that were "internal" for them at the time that they had the beliefs in question. That is to say, the principles need not be principles that *they* could then have applied by reflecting upon their own states of mind. For the beliefs make use of information that is now available to *us* and was not then available to them. Hence they do not tell us anything about what they were then justified in believing about themselves. So far as they were then concerned the beliefs were "external"; they could not apply the principles merely by reflecting upon their states of mind. But if *we* are able to use the principles to appraise the beliefs of others, then the principles do presuppose something about what *we* are internally justified in believing about *them*.

According to this traditional conception of "internal" epistemic justification, there is no *logical* connection between epistemic justification and truth. A belief may be internally justified and yet be *false*. This consequence is not acceptable to the externalist. He feels that an adequate account of epistemic justification should exhibit *some* logical connection between epistemic justification and *truth*.

In recent years there have been many proposals as to how epistemic justification might be explicated externally. But these suggestions, so far as I have been able to see, are of two sorts: either (1) they are empty or (2) they can be made to work only if they are supplemented by *internal* justification concepts. If this is true, then it has not yet been shown that internal concepts may be *replaced* by external ones.

I will consider, then, a number of externalistic attempts to explicate, "S is epistemically justified in believing p." I will suggest that some of them are empty (an "empty" explication being one that reduces justified belief to true belief). Then I will ask, with respect to those external explications that are not empty, whether they are adequate as they stand or whether they require supplementation by some epistemic concept that has not been shown to be externalistic.

THE NON-THEORY

I begin with a definition of external justification that is obviously unsatisfactory. I will use it to measure *other* possible definitions. For we may ask whether they tell us anything more than *it* does. We consider, then, theory (N)—"the non-theory":

(N)   S is externally justified in believing p = Df   p is true; and S is a thinking subject

The effect of this definition is to equate "external justification" with truth. Or, more exactly, the definition makes no distinction between the *true* beliefs that a person has and those beliefs that he is *justified* in having. I think it is fair to call this theory empty, since it does not contribute anything of significance to the theory of knowledge.

Can we, then, find a concept of "external" justification which does *not* thus reduce external justification to truth? Two types of external theory have been proposed—*reliability* theories and *causal* theories. And these may be combined into *mixed* reliability and causal theories.

I now turn to reliability theories.

RELIABILITY THEORIES OF EXTERNAL JUSTIFICATION

A common "reliability" definition of "external justification" is the following.[3]

[3]Compare Alvin Goldman: "Beliefs are justified if and only if they are produced by (relatively) reliable belief-forming processes." Op. cit., p. 47.

(R1)   S is externally justified in believing p = Df   The process by means of
            which S was led to believe p is reliable

One serious difficulty with the definition, as it stands, is that it does not
allow us to say, of a person who does not believe p, that he is justified in
believing p. But conceivably, by making judicious use of counterfactuals,
one could repair the definition to provide for this possibility.

A more serious difficulty has to do with the interpretation of the
expression "reliable process." If we take "process" in its broadest sense,
then we may say that a *process* by means of which one is led to a belief is a
series of *activities* that result in one's acquiring or retaining that belief. If we
understand "process" this way and if "reliable process" means no more
than, "process that is productive of true belief," then (R1) does not differ
from (N)—that is to say, the present version of the reliability theory does
not differ from the non-theory. For if the belief is true, then the process
that led to it, however bizarre the process may have been, produced a belief
that is true.

One may now want to say:

(R2)   S is externally justified in believing p = Df   The process by means of
            which S was led to believe p is a process which generally leads to true
            belief.

Does this add anything to (N)? If S has acquired a true belief, then once
again, no matter how bizarre the situation may be, he has followed *some*
procedure which is such that following that procedure *always* leads to true
belief.[4] Let us consider this point in more detail.

If a person S has arrived at a true belief on a particular occasion, then S
will have followed *some* procedure which was *unique* to that occasion. For
example, S could have arrived at his belief by reading the tea leaves on a
Friday afternoon twenty-seven minutes after having visited his uncle. If
necessary, we may add further specifications—say, something about what S
has just eaten or about the clothes that he is wearing. Since he has used this
successful procedure only on *one* occasion, we may say:

(e)   S has arrived at the belief that p by means of a belief-forming process
           which is such that, whenever he arrives at a belief by means of that process,
           the belief he thus arrives at is true

If what we have said is correct, then *every* belief that S has arrived at will be
one that has been arrived at by a unique process of the sort that (e)
describes. Hence there is a process which is equivalent to the disjunction of

---

[4]See the discussion of this general question in Richard Feldman, "Reliability and Justification," *The Monist*. Vol. 68 (1985), pp. 159–174.

all those successful belief-forming processes and which has provided S with as many justified beliefs as he has true beliefs.

We have, then, a counter-example to the analysis set forth in R2. It may seem, at first consideration, that a simple repair will save the definition. To see that this is so, consider the following dialogue between the reliabilist (R) and the internalist (I):

(R) "You need only specify that the process not be a disjunctive process."

(I) "A *disjunction* is a type of sentence; but what is it for a *process* to be disjunctive?"

(R) "A process is disjunctive if it can be described using disjunctive sentences."

(I) "But *every* process can be described using disjunctive sentences; and therefore, if what you say is right, *every* process is disjunctive."

(R) "No. What I mean is that a disjunctive process is a process that can be described *only* by using disjunctive sentences."

(I) "But there is *no* process which can be described *only* by using disjunctive sentences . . . [5]

The problem is that the following two propositions are true: (1) any disjunction of particular-procedures is such that, if we know enough about it, we can show it *also* to be a particular-procedure; and (2) any particular-procedure is such that, if we know enough about it, we can show it *also* to be a disjunction of particular-procedures. If you describe for me a procedure which you think is a disjunction of particular-procedures, I can add details which will entitle us to call it a particular-procedure, and if you describe for me a procedure which you think is a particular-procedure, I can add details which will entitle us to call it a disjunction of particular-procedures.

These observations are not intended to belittle the concept of a *reliable belief-forming process*. They are intended, rather, to belittle the suggestion that epistemic justification can be *defined* merely by reference to such processes. Obviously one should try to *know* what belief-forming processes one is following and one should try to *find out* which of those processes are

[5]In *Epistemology and Cognition* (Cambridge, MA: Harvard University Press, 1985), Alvin Goldman suggests other moves that the reliabilist might make to repair R2. Thus the somewhat bizarre example of the tea leaf reader could be avoided if we restricted our description of belief-forming processes to *organic processes* within the body of the believer (see p. 50). But here, too, there will be a unique bodily process for every belief-acquisition. We can all now truly say: "I never was in exactly *this* bodily state before and I never will be in it again." Should we add, then, that the processes be processes that are *relevant* to the acquisition or retention of belief? This move, of course, transfers the problem to that of finding a suitable analysis of "relevant."

reliable; then one should try as far as possible to follow them. But this is to say that we should be concerned to follow those processes which are such that we are *justified* in believing them to be reliable.

Consider, now, the following definition:

(R3)   S is externally justified in believing p = Df   The process by means of which S was led to believe p is one which is such that it is *evident* to S that that process generally leads to true belief

Since "evident" expresses one of the internalist's epistemic concepts and since no externalistic explication of the concept of *being evident* is at hand, we may say this of (R3): it is an analysis of external justification which *combines* internal and external justification concepts. We could replace "evident" in (R3) by "knows" and say that the process is one which is such that S *knows* that it generally leads to true belief. If no externalistic explication of knowledge is added, then, once again, we have a definition that *combines* internal and external concepts.

Another possibility is to construe a *reliable* process as a process which is *probably* such that it leads to truth.[6] Then we might have:

(R4)   S is externally justified in believing p = Df   The process by means of which S was led to believe p is a process which is *probably* such as to lead to true belief.

We have discussed in detail the *epistemic* concept of probability: the concept we have discussed is externalistic. Principle R4 has a certain plausibility if we take the word "probably" in this epistemic sense. But how is the principle to be applied if we take "probably" in its *external* sense? The difficulty may be seen by contrasting two of the principal uses of "probable"—the *statistical* use and the *relational* use.[7]

Statements in which "probable" is taken merely *statistically* are reword-

---

[6]Laurence Bonjour writes: "If finding epistemically justified beliefs did not substantially increase the likelihood of finding true ones, then epistemic justification would be irrelevant to our main cognitive goal and of dubious worth"; *The Structure of Empirical Knowledge* (Cambridge, MA: Harvard University Press, 1985), p. 8. Compare Ernest Sosa: "Faculty F is *more reliable* than faculty F' if the *likelihood* with which F would enable one to discriminate truth from falsehood in f (F) is higher than the likelihood with which F' would enable one to make such discrimination in f(F')." I have italicized "likelihood." (It should be noted that Sosa here speaks of faculties instead of belief-yielding processes.) See Ernest Sosa, "Knowledge and Intellectual Virtue," *The Monist*, Vol. 68 (1985), pp. 226–247; the quotation is on p. 238.

[7]See Rudolf Carnap, *Logical Foundations of Probability* (Chicago, IL: The University of Chicago Press, 1950), p. 300ff. Carnap speaks of statistical probability statements as statements about "probability^2: and of relational probability statements as statements about "probability^1". He notes that "under certain conditions, probability^1 may be regarded as an estimate of probability^2" (p. 300). But in the theory of knowledge, statements of relational probability are not concerned merely with estimates of relative frequencies; a typical statement of relational probability would be: "Thinking that one remembers p tends to make p probable."

ings of statements about statistical frequencies; they state what proportion of the members of one class are also members of another class. For example, "The probability that any given A is a B is n," might be interpreted as telling us, "n percent of the members of the class of A's are also members of the class of B's." (Statisticians make use of interpretations that are considerably more complex, but the added complexity does not affect the points that are here at issue.) What do statements about statistical frequencies tell us about the justification of belief?

It would not be helpful to say merely that a belief is justified provided only that it is a member of a set of beliefs most of whose members are *true*. For this would have the consequence that every belief is justified. Moreover, it would not help us find a plausible interpretation of R4. Our subject S had followed a belief-forming process which was such that *all* the beliefs that he arrived at by using that process were true. Hence the statistical probability of that process yielding a true belief would be a probability of 1. Taking explication (R4) this way, we do not progress beyond the original explication (N).

Or could the reliabilist take probability in its *relational* sense—in the sense of, "h is probable in relation to e"? We have seen how the concept of the *evident* may be used in explicating the application of this relational concept to the beliefs of a particular subject. But if the reliabilist does not make use of the concept of the evident how will *he* apply the relational concept?

Perhaps he will say this, "A proposition h is probable *for* a particular subject S, provided only: there is a *true* proposition e which is such that h is probable in relation to e and S accepts e." May we say of the proposition p, which S had arrived at as a result of his bizarre belief-forming process, that there *is* a *true* proposition which is such that p is more probable than not in relation to that proposition? One such proposition is our earlier proposition (e):

(e)   S has arrived at the belief that p by means of a belief-forming process which is such that, whenever he arrives at a belief by means of that process, the belief he thus arrives at is true

And so we have not found any purely external sense of "probability" in terms of which we can interpret the reliabilist's R4.

There are, of course, other statistical and relational interpretations of "probable," but, so far as I have been able to see, none of them is of any help to the externalist.[8]

---

[8]As we have seen, some would interpret the relational sense of "probability" without appeal to the concept of evidence and would say that a proposition is probable for a given person provided only that the proposition is probable in relation to what that person happens to *believe*. It is difficult to see how *this* way of construing probability would provide us with an account of epistemic justification.

CAUSAL THEORIES OF EXTERNAL JUSTIFICATION

Some have hoped to establish a connection between justification and truth by defining justification by reference to causation. Consider, for example, those true propositions which are such that their *being true* is what causes us to *believe* that they are true. Could it be that these are the propositions we are "externally" justified in believing? At best, this suggestion gives us a very restricted account of epistemic justification. For it is not applicable as it stands to propositions about the future. And it is doubtful whether it would be applicable to propositions that are logically true. Are there, however, *some* propositions that may be said to be justified in this way?

The locution, "A causes B," may be taken in two quite different ways—(1) as telling us that A is *the cause* of B or (2) as telling us that A *contributes causally* to B (that A is one of the *causal factors* that lead to B). We have, then, two causal definitions to consider.

The first is this:

(C1)   S is externally justified in believing p = Df   S believes p; and p's being true is *the cause* of S's believing p

The phrase "the cause" is certainly one that is in common use; indeed it is suggested by the familiar propositional connective, "because." Thus many people like to think that, of the various events that contribute causally to a given event, there is just one of them may properly be singled out as *the* cause of that event. Such a view is especially tempting when we are looking for a scapegoat.[9] But, as we know from the study of the nature of causation, the expression, "A is *the cause* of B," is one that is applicable only in very restricted circumstances and is not likely to be of use in connection with the present problem. If p, for example, is the proposition that there are mountains on the other side of the moon, then it is doubtful whether one could pick out *any* situation in which p's being true could be said to be *the cause* of anyone's belief that p. That event which is p's being true is just one of many factors which, working together, contribute causally to the belief that p.

What if we were to define, "A is *the cause* of B," by saying, "Of those events that contribute causally to E, A is the sole change that immediately preceded the occurrence of E"?[10] If we take "the cause" this way, then the

---

[9]We might say of the expression "the cause" what William James said of "cause"—namely that it is "an altar to an unknown God, an empty pedestal still marking the place of a hoped for statue." William James, *The Principles of Psychology* (New York: Henry Holt and Company, 1893), Vol. II, p. 671.

[10]C. J. Ducasse proposed that "the cause of a change K" is that change which "alone occurred in the immediate environment of K immediately before"; *Truth, Knowledge and Causation* (London: Routledge & Kegan Paul, 1968), p. 4. Ducasse's definition, unlike the one proposed above, did not make use of the concept of causal contribution (causal factor).

cause of the acquisition of a belief might be some other psychological event (the occurrence, say, of a certain thought) or it might be some neuro-physiological event. Application of (C1), therefore, would be restricted to those beliefs which are about such psychological or neuro-physiological events.

Does the causal theory fare better if we replace "is the cause of" by "causally contributes to"? Then we would have:

(C2)   S is externally justified in believing p = Df   S believes p; and p's being true *contributes causally* to S's believing p

Now the definition is subject to Rube Goldberg counter-examples. Consider a person who is working in the garden and who suddenly becomes tired. His fatigue leads him to go inside and read the newspaper. He reads that some of the people who suffer from a certain internal disorder have red hair. Since *he* has red hair and is also a hypochondriac, he concludes, "*I've* got that disorder!" If, now, his having that disorder was one of the many factors that contributed causally to his fatigue, then we may say that, according to (C2), he is externally justified in believing that he has that disorder. *This* concept of justification is not likely to be of use in investigating the theory of knowledge.

Could one overcome such difficulties by specifying a type of causation that is not transitive? *Direct causation* is not transitive. (Roughly, "A is a direct causal contributor to B, if and only if: A contributes causally to B, and A does not contribute causally to anything that contributes causally to B.") The direct contributor to a belief attribution would then presumably be either another psychological state or an internal physiological state. This move, then, has the same difficulties as the version of "the cause" move considered above.

Our example above may suggest that the subject S should be *aware of* the causal role that is played by *p* in the formation of his belief. And so one might suggest:

(C3)   S is externally justified in believing p = Df   S believes p; p's being true contributes causally to S's believing p; and it is *evident* to S that p's being true contributes causally to his belief that p

This proposal is like R3 above: it *combines* internal and external justification concepts.[11]

---

[11]This type of theory is suggested by Marshall Swain who proposes a causal theory that makes use of such internalistic expressions as the following: "S's evidence" and "renders evident." See Marshall Swain, "Knowledge, Causality and Justification," in Pappas and Swain, op. cit., pp. 87–99.

MIXED THEORIES

The reliability and causal theories that we have considered may be combined in various ways.[12] We need consider only two possibilities:

(M1)   S is externally justified in believing p = Df   S believes that p; and *the cause* of S's believing that p is that S follows a belief-forming process that *generally leads to true belief*

This combines R2 and C1 and obviously has the difficulties of each.

(M2)   S is externally justified in believing p = Df   S believes that p; and one of the facts that *contributes causally* to his believing p is the fact that he followed a belief-forming process which, *more probably than not*, yields true belief

This combines R4 and C2 and obviously has the difficulties of each.

The "externalistic" explications of epistemic justification that we have considered are all such that either they are empty or they make use of internal concepts. It would seem, therefore, that there is no indication that externalistic justification concepts may *replace* internal concepts.

---

[12]"*Reliabilism* is the view that a belief is epistemically justified if and only if it is *produced* or *sustained* by a cognitive process that reliably yields truth and avoids error." Sosa, op. cit., p. 239. I have italicized the causal expressions "produced" and "sustained."

CHAPTER 9

Foundationalism and the Coherence Theory

THE SOURCES OF JUSTIFICATION

According to the concept of knowledge that has been developed here, the epistemic status of an empirical belief is a function of three different things.

(1) The object of a belief may be self-presenting. In such a case, the belief may be called a *basic apprehension*.

(2) Some beliefs have a kind of *prima facie* probability. If I accept a proposition, and if that proposition is not disconfirmed by my total evidence, then it is that proposition is probable for me.

And, finally, (3) a belief may derive its epistemic status from the way in which it logically *concurs* with the other things one believes. As we have seen, these relations may raise the level of the proposition believed from that of being merely probable to that of being evident.

The present account of knowledge is appropriately called *foundational*, since it includes basic apprehensions among the sources of epistemic justification.[1] And it may also be called *coherence theory* since it includes mutual

[1]The "common sense" aspect of the present view—namely, its emphasis upon *prima facie* probabilities—has also been called "foundational." But if we use "foundational" in this broader way, we should take care not to confuse *prima facie* probabilities with basic apprehensions. The fact that a religious belief, for example, is *prima facie* probable should not be taken to mean that the belief is a basic apprehension. This point is relevant to the questions discussed by Alvin Plantinga in "Reason and Belief in God," in Alvin Plantinga and Nicholas Wolterstorff, eds., *Faith and Rationality* (Notre Dame, IN: University of Notre Dame Press, 1983), pp. 16–93. Compare Robert Audi, "Psychological Foundationalism," *The Monist*, Vol.

support among the sources of epistemic justification. It would be a mistake, therefore, to say that foundational theories and coherence theories of epistemic justification must be incompatible. (This is not to deny, of course, that different theories may place different emphases on the roles to be placed by basic apprehensions and by mutual support.)[2] Yet it has been contended (1) that *no* foundational theory is possible and (2) that coherence theories need not be foundational.

Let us consider these contentions in turn.

IS FOUNDATIONALISM IMPOSSIBLE?

One could prove that foundationalism is impossible if one could prove that basic apprehensions are impossible. Laurence Bonjour has constructed the following argument to prove that basic apprehensions—in his terms, "basic empirical beliefs"—are impossible.[3]

(1) Suppose that there are *basic empirical beliefs*, that is, empirical beliefs (a) which are epistemically justified and (b) whose justification does not depend on that of any further empirical beliefs.
(2) For a belief to be epistemically justified requires that there be a reason why it is likely to be true.
(3) For a belief to be epistemically justified for a particular person requires that this person be himself in cognitive possession of such a reason.
(4) The only way to be in cognitive possession of such a reason is to believe *with justification* the premises from which it follows that the belief is likely to be true.
(5) The premises of such a justifying argument for an empirical belief cannot be entirely *a priori*; at least one such premise must be empirical.

"Therefore"

(6) The justification of a supposed basic empirical belief must depend on the justification of at least one other empirical belief, contradicting (1).

Therefore

(7) There can be no basic empirical beliefs.

---

61 (1978), pp. 592–610. I believe that the view I have defended in the present book is what Audi would call "Modest Epistemic Psychological Foundationalism"; see pages 597 and 600 of his paper.

[2]Compare Ernest Sosa, "The Raft and the Pyramid," *Midwest Studies in Philosophy*, Vol. V (1980), pp. 3–25; and Susan Haack, "Theories of Knowledge: An Analytic Framework," *Proceedings of the Aristotelian Society*, Vol. 83 (1983), pp. 143–157.

[3]Laurence Bonjour, *The Structure of Empirical Knowledge* (Cambridge, MA: Cambridge University Press, 1985), p. 32. (I have altered the numbering of the final steps in the argument.) Compare Keith Lehrer's criticism of foundationalism in "The Coherence Theory of Knowledge," *Philosophical Topics*, Vol. XIV (1986), pp. 5–26; esp., pp. 20–21.

It is clear that the conclusion follows from the premises. Hence, if we reject the conclusion, we must find a problem with at least one of the premises. And this is not difficult, for we do not need to go beyond premise (2).

The word "likely" is an alternative to "probable." And the word "probable," as we have seen, may be taken either externally or internally. Taken externally, "probable" tells us something about statistical frequencies or numerical proportions. Taken internally it tells us something about epistemic justification. We have said that a proposition is probable for a given subject S provided only that S is more justified in believing the proposition than he or she is in believing its negation. How, then, are we to take "likely" in the above argument?

If we take "likely" in its *external* sense, then premise (3) is false. A belief may be epistemically justified for a person even though that person is not "in cognitive possession" of any proposition about statistical frequencies. And if we take "likely" in its *internal* sense, then premise (2) is false. A belief in what is self-presenting may be justified even though no *other* belief constitutes a reason for thinking it to be true.

IS A NONFOUNDATIONAL COHERENCE THEORY POSSIBLE?

To see the difficulties involved in developing a nonfoundational coherence theory of epistemic justification, let us consider once again the nature of mutual support.

The following is a set of propositions that mutually support each other:

(e)   Most of those who have read this book are philosophers; and David has read this book if and only if John has read this book
(h)   David has read this book and is a philosopher
(i)   John has read this book and is a philosopher

Any two of these propositions together confirm the third; in other words, each of the three propositions is probable in relation to the conjunction of the other two. Thus e&h, for example, confirms i: if e and h were the only evidence you had that was relevant to i, then i would be probable for you (you would be more justified in accepting i than in accepting not-i). Similarly, e&i confirms h, and h&i confirms e. Here, then, we have a clear case of that *logical* relation that we have called the "mutual support" of propositions—a relation that could also be called the "mutual coherence" of propositions.

How are we to *apply* the relation to the beliefs of a particular subject S? The coherence theorist may wish to say that, if a person S accepts three propositions that are thus related by mutual support, then the three propositions mutually support each other *for* S. The theory would thus be somewhat latitudinarian at the outset, just as our theory was somewhat latitudinarian at the outset. The coherence theorist may then hope to tighten up his or her requirements at a later stage.

But it is very difficult to see where the coherentist could go from this point. To understand the difficulty, we should consider two facts about the confirmation relation, "h is probable in relation to e (e confirms h)." One is that, if the confirmation relation is to be *applied* to the epistemic situation of a particular subject S, then the *confirming* proposition e must be *evident* for S. And the other is that application of the confirmation relation allows us to say, of the *confirmed* proposition h, only that it is *probable* for S. How, then, is the coherentist to proceed if he or she does not appeal to basic apprehensions? What will his or her *next* step be?

These are not easy questions to answer.

Many coherent theorists seem to believe, nevertheless, that they can develop a nonfoundational coherence theory of epistemic justification— even though no one has ever shown just *how* this might be done.[4] Possibly these coherentists are making a move like the one that we had made when, in the first chapter of this book, we considered what to say about the skeptic's objection: they are *withholding* commitment to the proposition that they can succeed. And so, for the moment, let us also withhold belief with respect to the proposition that they can succeed.

We will suppose, then, that some of the confirming propositions that are probable for S can make *other* propositions probable for S. Is the coherentist now entitled to go on and say that those other propositions, in turn, can then go on to make still *further* propositions probable for S?

To see that he or she is not entitled to do this, we have only to note that the confirmation relation—the relation expressed by, "h is probable in relation to e"—is not transitive.[5] That is to say, from the facts that (i) B is probable in relation to A, (ii) C is probable in relation to B, and (iii) D is probable in relation to C, it does not follow that (iv) D is probable in relation to A.

To see that this is so, consider the following propositions:

(1)   Most A's are B's; most B's are C's; most C's are D's; and x is an A
(2)   Most A's are B's; most B's are C's; most C's are D's; and x is a B
(3)   Most A's are B's; most B's are C's; most C's are D's; and x is a C
(4)   Most A's are B's; most B's are C's; most C's are D's; and x is a D

---

[4]Bonjour concedes that a coherence theory should satisfy an "Observation Requirement": the theory must contain "laws attributing a high degree of reliability to a reasonable variety of cognitively spontaneous beliefs (including in particular those kinds of introspective beliefs which are required for the recognition of other cognitively spontaneous beliefs" (*The Structure of Empirical Knowledge*, p. 141). But Bonjour gives no indication as to how his program might be carried out without basic apprehensions.

[5]In this respect, the confirmation relation differs from the *tending-to-make-evident* relation ("e tends to make h evident") and from the applied *making-evident* relation ("e makes h evident for S").

We may say that (1) confirms (2), that (2) confirms (3), and that (3) confirms (4). But we may *not* say that (3) confirms (4).

An example may be clearer. A is the surface of a chessboard and thus contains 64 squares; B is a subsurface of A that contains 36 squares; C is a subsurface of B that contains 25 squares; and D is a subsurface of C that contains 9 squares. Clearly, most of the squares in A are in B, most of the squares in B are in C, and most of the squares in C are in D. But it is not the case that most of the squares in A are in D.

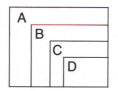

The accompanying diagram may be more intuitive.

Constructing a coherence theory of justification without making use of basic apprehensions is not unlike recording your new song by taping other recordings and without ever having given a live performance. I think we may safely conclude that any adequate theory of knowledge and epistemic justification requires basic apprehensions as well as mutual support.

CHAPTER 10

What Is Knowledge?

THE PROBLEM OF THE THEAETETUS

If you know that it is raining, then it *is* raining and you *believe* that it is raining. The point may be generalized by saying that, if you have knowledge, then you have true belief. But knowledge is more than mere true belief. For your belief that it is raining could be true even if you didn't *know* that it is raining. Perhaps you have simply made a lucky guess. What, then, must be *added* to true belief to get knowledge? Finding the answer to this question is sometimes called, "the problem of the *Theaetetus*," since the question was first clearly formulated by Plato in his dialogue of that name.

The traditional or classic answer—and the one proposed in Plato's dialogue, the *Theaetetus*—is that knowledge is *justified* true belief. The relevant sense of "justified" is the one we have expressed by means of the term "evident"; knowledge is *evident* true belief. According to this conception of knowledge, three conditions must obtain if a person knows a proposition to be true. First, the proposition is true; secondly, the person accepts it; and, thirdly, the proposition is one that is evident for that person.[1] Hence the classical definition of knowledge may be put this way:

S knows that h is true = Df   h is true; S accepts h; and h is evident for S.

---

[1]Some philosophers have suggested that a proposition might be known without being accepted. For criticisms of this suggestion, see Keith Lehrer, *Knowledge* (Oxford: The Clarendon Press, 1974), Chapter 3, and D. W. Armstrong, *Belief, Truth and Knowledge* (Cambridge: Cambridge University Press, 1973), 137–149.

THE GETTIER PROBLEM

We have seen that a belief may be both evident and *false*. In countenancing the possibility that a proposition *e* may *inductively*, or *nondemonstratively*, confer evidence upon a proposition *h*, we have also countenanced the possibility that in such a case *e* is true and *h* is false. This means that, for all we know, some of the propositions that are evident to us are also false. But if this is possible, then the traditional definition must be modified.

This problem for the traditional definition of knowledge was first noted by Edmund L. Gettier in a paper entitled "Is Justified True Belief Knowledge?" published in 1963.[2] The problem has since become known, appropriately, as, "the Gettier problem." It is also called, "the problem of the fourth condition," since it leads one to ask, "Is there some suitable fourth condition which may be added to the three that are set forth in the traditional definition of knowledge?"

Gettier noted that the following situation, among others, is counter to the traditional definition of knowledge:

> Let us suppose that Smith has strong evidence for the following proposition:
>
> (f)   Jones owns a Ford.
>
> Smith's evidence might be that Jones has at all times in the past within Smith's memory owned a car, and always a Ford, and that Jones has just offered Smith a ride while driving a Ford. Let us imagine, now, that Smith has another friend, Brown, of whose whereabouts he is totally ignorant. Smith selects three place names quite at random, and constructs the following three propositions:
>
> (g)   Either Jones owns a Ford, or Brown is in Boston;
>
> (h)   Either Jones owns a Ford, or Brown is in Barcelona;
>
> (i)   Either Jones owns a Ford, or Brown is in Brest-Litovsk.
>
> Each of these propositions is entailed by (f). Imagine that Smith realized the entailment of each of these propositions he has constructed by (f), and proceeds to accept (g), (h), and (i) on the basis of (f). Smith has correctly inferred (g), (h), and (i) from a proposition for which he has strong evidence. Smith is therefore completely justified in believing each of these three propositions. Smith, of course, has no idea where Brown is.
>
> But imagine now that two further conditions hold. First, Jones does *not* own a Ford, but is at present driving a rented car. And secondly, by the sheerest coincidence, and entirely unknown to Smith, the place mentioned in proposition (h) happens really to be the place where Brown is. If these two conditions hold then Smith does *not* know that (h) is true, even though (*i*) (h) is true, (*ii*) Smith does believe that (h) is true, and (*iii*) Smith is justified in believing that (h) is true.[3]

[2]Edmund L. Gettier, "Is Justified True Belief Knowledge?" *Analysis*, Vol. 23 (1963), pp. 121–123.

[3]*Op. cit.*, pp. 122–123.

Gettier concludes, therefore, that the traditional definition of knowledge does not give us a *sufficient* reason for saying that someone knows a given proposition to be true. The person Smith and the proposition (h) of Gettier's example satisfy the conditions of the traditional definition. For (1) the proposition that either Jones owns a Ford or Brown is in Barcelona is true, (2) Smith accepts the proposition that either Jones owns a Ford or Brown is in Barcelona, and (3) it is evident for Smith that either Jones owns a Ford or Brown is in Barcelona. But it is clear that, in the situation Gettier describes, Smith does not *know* that either Jones owns a Ford or Brown is in Barcelona.

Gettier was the first philosopher to see that the traditional definition of knowledge is thus inadequate. Since the publication of his now classic paper in 1963, many other counter-examples to the traditional definition have been formulated, most of them not different in principle from the one just cited.

Once Gettier had pointed out the inadequacy of the traditional definition, it became apparent that certain other cases which had puzzled earlier philosophers could also have been used to show that the traditional definition requires modification. We will mention two of these: one suggested by A. Meinong in 1906, the other by Bertrand Russell in 1948.

Meinong considers an Austrian garden where there is an Aeolian harp made to whistle in the wind and thereby keep the birds away. "Assume now," he says, "that someone who has lived in the vicinity of such an apparatus has become hard of hearing in the course of time and has developed a tendency to have auditory hallucinations. It could easily happen that he hallucinates the familiar sounds of the Aeolian harp at the very moment at which these sounds are actually to be heard."[4] If this were to happen, then, given the theory of perception set forth in the present work, one might say that the man had a true and evident belief to the effect that the harp was then sounding. But it hardly would be true to say that he thereby *knew* that the harp was then sounding.

Russell wrote:

It is very easy to give examples of true beliefs that are not knowledge. There is the man who looks at a clock which is not going, though he thinks it is, and who happens to look at it the moment when it is right; this man acquires a true belief as to the time of day, but cannot be said to have knowledge. There is the man who believes, truly, that the last name of the Prime Minister in 1906 began with a B, but who believes this because he thinks that Balfour was Prime Minister then, whereas it was Campbell Bannerman.[5]

---

[4]A. Meinong, *Über die Erfahrungsgrundlagen unseres Wissens* (1906). Meinong constructs cites another example, involving a man who is disturbed by a ringing in his ears at a time when, as luck would have it, someone happens to be ringing the doorbell. The two examples may be found in Volume V of the Meinong *Gesamtausgabe* (Graz: Akademische Druck- und Verlagsanstalt, 1973), pp. 398-399, 619.

[5]Bertrand Russell, *Human Knowledge: Its Scope and Limits* (New York: Simon and Schuster, 1948), p. 155.

(Russell's second man may be compared with those supporters of George McGovern who believed, in 1972, that Nixon's successor would be a man whose first name began with "G.") If we add, in these cases, that the true propositions in question are also evident, then these cases are counter to the traditional definition of knowledge.

Consider a slightly different example. A person *takes* there to be a sheep in the field and does so under conditions which are such that, when under those conditions a person takes there to be a sheep in the field, then it is *evident* for that person that there is a sheep in the field. The person, however, has mistaken a dog for a sheep and so what he sees is not a sheep at all. Nevertheless it happens that there *is* a sheep in another part of the field. Hence, the proposition that there is a sheep in the field will be one that is both true and evident and it will also be one that the person accepts. But the situation does not warrant our saying that the person *knows* that there is a sheep in the field.

A NOTE OF CAUTION

Many of the examples that have been discussed in connection with the Gettier problem would seem *not* to be cases where the evidence justifies something false. One of the clearest and most influential of such examples was proposed by Alvin Goldman. Suppose, he suggests, that Henry is driving through the countryside and sees a barn a few feet away. It looks just as one would expect a barn to look. And so Henry has no reason to question his senses. He would seem to be justified in the true belief that there *is* a barn that he sees. But suppose further that

unknown to Henry, the district he has entered is full of papier-mâché facsimiles of barns. These facsimiles look from the road exactly like barns, but are really just facades, without back walls or interiors, quite incapable of being used as barns. Having just entered the district, Henry has not encountered any facsimiles; the object he sees is a genuine barn. But if the object on that site were a facsimile, Henry would mistake it for a barn.[6]

Henry, it would seem clear, has *justified true belief* that it is a barn that he sees, and yet he cannot be said to *know* that he sees a barn. And his evidence, we may assume, is not defective: it does not justify him in any *false* belief.

There is a serious problem with this example. Henry's true belief that he sees a barn, although it is a *justified* true belief, is not an *evident* true belief. His evidence may make it *probable* for him—indeed, his evidence may even make it *beyond reasonable doubt* for him—that he sees a barn. But nothing makes if *evident* for him that he sees a barn. For such a thing to be evident

[6]Alvin Goldman, "Discrimination and Perceptual Knowledge, *Journal of Philosophy*, Vol. 73 (1976), pp. 771–791; the example is on pages 772–773.

for him, as we have seen in discussing the evidence of the senses, Henry would need to have far more evidence then he now has. And if it is not evident to Henry that he sees a barn or that there is a barn there, then Henry does not *know* that he sees a barn or that there is a barn there.

The example makes clear, once again, the importance of distinguishing *levels* of epistemic justification.[7] And it reminds us, once again, that *justified* true belief need not be the *evident* true belief that is required by the concept of knowing.[8]

A CLOSER LOOK AT THE EXAMPLE

What may be said about Gettier's original example may also be applied, *mutatis mutandis*, to the other examples. In discussing how to deal with the problem, therefore, let us restrict ourselves to the original example.

At first consideration, the problem may seem easy to solve. But the easy answers will not work. Let us consider four such answers.

(1) The true proposition—"Jones owns a Ford or Brown is in Barcelona"—that constitutes a counter-example to the traditional definition of knowledge, is a proposition for which Smith has only inductive or non-demonstrative evidence. It is made evident for him by propositions that do not entail it. One may be tempted to say, therefore, that no such proposition can be known to be true. But, as we have seen, unless the things we can know are restricted to what is self-presenting or *a priori*, we must face the possibility that some of the things we know have only inductive, or non-demonstrative, evidence.

We will assume, then, that we do know such propositions as that expressed by, "Jones owns a Ford." And we will also assume that the kind of evidence we have for such propositions does not significantly differ in content from the kind of evidence that Gettier described.[9]

(2) The evidence e that Smith has for h (Jones owns a Ford or Smith is in

---

[7]Compare Robert Audi, "Defeated Knowledge, Reliability, and Justification," *Midwest Studies in Philosophy*, Vol. V (1980), pp. 75–96.

[8]In considering the example, one may be impressed by the epistemic distinction between the proposition (h), "Jones owns a Ford," and that proposition (i), "Jones keeps a Ford in his garage . . . " which makes h evident for Jones. The latter proposition is not *certain* for Jones and yet one has the feeling that it is of a higher epistemic order from Smith than the *evident* proposition that Jones owns a Ford. Our theory of epistemic categories may be said to confirm this feeling, since we have noted that the *obvious* falls between the certain and the evident.

[9]Actually the evidence e that Gettier cites ("Jones has at all times in the past within Smith's memory owned a car and always a Ford and Jones has just offered Smith a ride while driving a Ford") is not itself sufficient to make f evident for Smith. At most, they justify f only in the weaker sense of making h beyond reasonable doubt. In discussing the example, therefore, we will imagine that Smith's evidence e contains still other propositions (e.g., "Jones keeps a Ford in his garage," along with other such propositions) and that the whole conjunction of propositions does make f evident for Smith.

Barcelona) confers evidence upon the *false* proposition *f* (Jones owns a Ford). This fact has suggested to many that Gettier's problem may be dealt with in a very simple way: we have only to stipulate—they suppose—that if one is to have knowledge, then the evidence that one has must not confer evidence upon anything that is false. Such a stipulation would rule out too much. For Smith's evidence *e* is itself a proposition that he knows to be true and *e* makes *f* evident for him. Hence the proposed solution would require us to say, incorrectly, that Smith does not know *e* to be true.

We must, therefore, reconcile ourselves to the fact that a proposition *can* be known even though what confers evidence upon that proposition also confers evidence upon a proposition that is false.

(3) Gettier's Smith was lucky in the proposition that he had hit upon, "Either Jones owns a Ford or Brown is in Barcelona." This leads Alvin Goldman to observe, "One thing that seems to be missing in this example is a causal connection between the fact that makes *p* true [or simply, the fact that *p*] and S's belief that p."[10] Hence the following possibility suggests itself: we say that if a proposition is known, then the fact that the proposition is true is *causally connected* with the fact that the proposition is believed. But let us look at the suggestion more closely.

As we have seen in discussing "externalism," it is not easy to single out any one event as being *the* cause of a given occurrence. This is especially difficult when the occurrence is the acquisition of a belief. Normally the most that we can say is that this and that *contribute causally* to one's having the belief. Returning to Gettier's example, let us consider someone—say, Brown himself—who *does* know that either Jones owns a Ford or Brown is in Barcelona. There is no clear sense in which that disjunctive fact could be said to be *the* cause of Brown's having a belief that is directed upon it. And, indeed, it is problematic whether the disjunctive fact—as distinguished from the fact that Brown is in Barcelona—could even be said to *contribute causally* to Brown's belief.

"It is essential to Gettier's example, however, that Brown being in Barcelona does not even *contribute* causally to Smith having the belief that he has." Actually that is *not* essential to Gettier's example. Suppose that among the things that contributed causally to Smith's thinking of Barcelona and not, say, of Bratislava was the fact that he had overheard Robinson asking Miller whether Barcelona was in Spain. Suppose further that, among the things that contributed causally to Robinson's question, was the fact that, wholly unknown to Smith, Brown's wife has told Robinson that the weather is now ideal in Barcelona. And suppose, finally, that among the things contributing to her saying *that* was the fact that her husband has told her as much on the telephone. Such a causal connection between Smith's belief

---

[10]Alvin Goldman, "A Causal Theory of Knowing," George S. Pappas and Marshall Swain, eds., *Essays on Knowledge and Justification* (Ithaca, NY: Cornell University Press, 1978), pp. 67–86; the quotation is on page 68.

and Brown's being in Barcelona would not entitle us to say that Smith *knows* that either Jones owns a Ford or Brown is in Barcelona.

(4) One may be tempted to say, "Smith *would* have had the belief he had even if Brown had *not* been in Barcelona." And this counterfactual conditional suggests that there may be another way of dealing with the problem. Shall we consider saying that, in the case of knowledge, the proposition believed is one such that, if it had been *false*, then the person would *not* have accepted it? Robert Nozick has proposed such a counterfactual definition. According to him, "S knows that h," might be explicated in the following way, "S accepts h; h is true; and in arriving at his belief, S followed a method which is such that, if h had been false and S had followed that method, then S would not have accepted h."[11] Unfortunately, however, definition by means of counterfactual conditionals is somewhat risky, since such definitions are fairly easily brought down by means of examples which are themselves counterfactual.

The hope is to formulate a counterfactual definition of knowledge which is such that, in application to Gettier's example, it will *not* require us to say of Smith that he *knows* that either Jones owns a Ford or Brown is in Barcelona. In application to this case, Nozick's proposal is essentially this:

> S knows that either Jones owns a Ford or Brown is in Barcelona = Df
> (1)   S accepts the proposition that either Jones owns a Ford or Brown is in Barcelona; (2)   the proposition in question is true; and (3)   in arriving at his belief, S followed a method which is that, if the proposition had been false and S had followed that method, then S would not have accepted that proposition.

How is such a definition to be evaluated?

In testing a definition, we ask whether there are any possible circumstances under which the first part (the definiendum) would be true and the second part (the definiens) false; and we ask whether there are any possible circumstances under which the first part would be false and the second part true. Somewhat more exactly, we look for circumstances which are logically independent of each of the two parts of the definition and which are such that, under those circumstances, the one part of the definition would be true and the other part false. If we find no such circumstances, then we may hope, at least, that there are no such circumstances. But if we do find such a circumstance, then we will know that the definition is inadequate.

Let us look again at the definition proposed above. Are there any possible circumstances under which the three conditions of the definiens would be satisfied and S would *not* know that either Jones owns a Ford or Brown is in Barcelona? Clearly there are many such possible circumstances.

[11]See Robert Nozick, *Philosophical Explanations* (Cambridge, MA: Belknap Press, 1981), pp. 178–180. Nozick's definition is more complex than the one that I have formulated, but the added complexity does not affect the point that is here made.

One would be this: Smith is such that, if he had followed the method in question and Jones had not owned a Ford, then he, Smith, would have believed that Jones does not exist. Another would be this: if Smith had followed the method in question and Jones had not owned a Ford, then Smith would no longer have *any* beliefs. It is logically possible that such things *could* happen. And we could hardly say, in such cases, that Smith *knows* that either Jones owns a Ford or Brown is in Barcelona. And therefore the proposed counterfactual definition is inadequate.

Some philosophers, after reflection upon this problem, have despaired of providing any definition of knowledge at all and have suggested that perhaps the best we can do is merely to formulate certain necessary conditions of certain types of knowledge. But let us try to repair the traditional definition of knowledge.

A DEFINITION OF KNOWLEDGE

Many different repairs have been suggested, but unfortunately there is no consensus as to whether any of them has been successful. Some of them are very difficult to understand, for they go considerably beyond the store of concepts we have permitted ourselves in the present work.[12] We will not attempt to evaluate the various suggestions that have been made, but will simply ask whether the traditional definition can be repaired within the general scheme of concepts that we have been using.

Let us say that a "Gettier case" is a situation of this sort: there is a person who accepts a true proposition that is evident for him and the proposition is *not* one that he knows to be true. Let us now consider certain facts about the propositions that are thus involved in Gettier cases.

The propositions involved in Gettier cases are all such that they are made evident by *other* propositions. As we have seen, the relation of *making evident* is inductive, or nondemonstrative. This means that, if one proposition makes another evident, then the first proposition does not logically entail

[12]Among the more important earlier discussions of Gettier's article are: Keith Lehrer and Thomas Paxson, "Knowledge: Undefeated Justified True Belief," *Journal of Philosophy*, Vol. LXVI (1969), 225–237; Fred Dretske, "Conclusive Reasons, *Australasian Journal of Philosophy*, Vol. 49 (1971), 1–22; Peter D. Klein, "A Proposed Definition of Propositional Knowledge," *Journal of Philosophy*, Vol. LXIII (1971), 471–482; Bredo C. Johnsen, "Knowledge," *Philosophical Studies*, Vol. XXV (1974), 273–282; John L. Pollock, *Knowledge and Justification* (Princeton, NJ: Princeton University Press, 1974); Keith Lehrer, *Knowledge* (Oxford: The Clarendon Press, 1974); Marshall Swain, "Epistemic Defeasibility," *American Philosophical Quarterly*, XI (1974), 15-2; and Ernest Sosa, "How Do You Know?" *American Philosophical Quarterly*, Vol. XI (1974), pp. 113–122. Some of the classic attempts are published in Michael D. Roth and Leon Galis, *Knowing: Essays in the Analysis of Knowledge* (New York: Random House, 1970). For a detailed survey and examination of these and subsequent attempts to deal with Gettier's problem, see Robert K. Shope, *The Analysis of Knowing: A Decade of Research* (Princeton, NJ: Princeton University Press, 1983).

the second proposition. And therefore it is possible for a true proposition to make a *false* proposition evident.

The various Gettier cases also have this feature in common: the proposition involved is made evident by a proposition that makes some *false* proposition evident.[13] Hence they are all cases of what may be said, in the following sense, to be "defectively evident":

D1   h is defectively evident for S = Df   (1)   There is an e such that e makes h evident for S; and (2)   everything that makes h evident for S makes something that is false evident for S

The expression, "e makes h evident for h," should, of course, be taken in the way defined in Chapter 6.[14]

The proposition "Jones owns a Ford or Brown is in Barcelona" is defectively evident for Smith. It is made evident for S by the proposition e ("Jones has at all times kept a Ford in his garage . . . etc."), and *everything* that makes e evident for Smith also makes a false proposition evident for Smith—namely, the proposition that Jones owns a Ford. (In considering this fact, one should keep in mind what was said in Chapter 6—that no proposition makes itself evident. Hence "Jones owns a Ford" does *not* make itself evident.)

Shall we, then, add "h is not defectively evident" as the fourth condition of our definition of knowledge? This would not be quite enough. For, if we were to do this, then we would have to say, incorrectly, that Gettier's Smith does *not* know that e ("Jones has at all times in the past . . . etc.") is true. For e, like h, is defectively evident by our definition. So we must make the definition slightly more complicated.

The conjuncts of e (e.g., "Jones keeps a Ford in his garage"), unlike e itself, are *not* defectively evident. Although in conjunction they make a false proposition evident, none of them by itself makes a false proposition evident. This fact suggests the following definition:

D2   h is known by S = Df   (1) h is true; (2) S accepts h; (3) h is evident for S; and (4) if h is defectively evident for S, then h is implied by a conjunction of propositions each of which is evident for S but not defectively evident for S

---

[13]This general diagnosis of the problem is also suggested by: Keith Lehrer, in "Self-Profile" (pp. 91–96) in Radu J. Bogdan, ed., *Keith Lehrer*; and Ernest Sosa, in *"Presuppositions of Empirical Knowledge," Philosophical Papers*, Vol. XV (1986), pp. 75–88.

[14]Give n an analysis (which, unfortunately, we do not have) of what is meant by "S accepts h for the wrong reasons," we could add a further condition to our definiens and say that S does *not* accept h "for the wrong reasons." As we shall see, however, it is not clear that such a stipulation is required for defining what it is to *know*—as distinguished from what it is to have *insight* into what one knows.

We have, then, a proposed solution to Gettier's complication of the problem of the *Theaetetus*. The solution is not simple, but it is much more simple than many of its alternatives. And, like those alternatives we have criticized, our definition has the virtue that, if it *is* wrong, then one can show precisely at what point an error was made.[15]

KNOWING THAT ONE KNOWS

Does knowing include knowing that one knows?

The principle according to which *knowing* that h includes *knowing that one knows* that h is one that Hintikka has appropriately called "the KK principle" and it has been affirmed by many philosophers.[16] Thus Schopenhauer said:

Your knowing that you know differs only in words from your knowing. 'I know that I know' means nothing more than 'I know,' . . . If your knowing and your knowing that you know are two different things, just try to separate them, and first to know without knowing that you know, then to know that you know without this knowledge being at the same time knowing.[17]

Is the KK principle true?

If I know that I know a certain proposition h, then it is *evident to me that h is evident* to me.[18] Shall we say, then, that if a proposition is evident, then it is also evident that it is evident? Or that, if a proposition is evident, then it is evident that it is known?

A proposition cannot be evident to a person unless the person understands the proposition. Now it is possible that there is a person who does not yet have the concept of evidence or of knowledge, but for whom, all the same, a certain proposition is known. Such a person, then, would be one for whom it would not be evident that anything is known or evident. Therefore a proposition may be evident without it being evident that it is

---

[15]I am indebted to many philosophers for criticisms of earlier versions of this solution. Of these philosophers, Earl Conee deserves special mention.

[16]Jaakko Hintikka, *Knowledge and Belief* (Ithaca, NY: Cornell University Press, 1962); Hintikka also affirms a version of this principle. Compare: E. J. Lemmon, "If I Know, Do I Know That I Know?", in Avrum Stroll, ed., *Epistemology: New Essays in the Theory of Knowledge* (New York: Harper & Row, 1967), 54–82; Carl Ginet, "What Must be Added to Knowing to Obtain Knowing that One Knows," *Synthese*, Vol. XXI (1970), 163–186; and Risto Hilpinen, "Knowing that One Knows and the Classical Definition of Knowledge," *Synthese*," Vol. XXI (1970), 109–132.

[17]Arthur Schopenhauer, *The Fourfold Root of Sufficient Reason* (London: George Bell and Sons, 1897), Section 41, 166.

[18]Compare John Pollock: "Whenever *h* is evident for a person, then it is also evident for him that he knows *h*." From "Chisholm's Definition of Knowledge," *Philosophical Studies*, XIX (1968), 72–76; the quotation is on p. 74.

evident, and a proposition may be known without it being known that it is known.[19]

We should not say, then, that knowing implies knowing that one knows. Shall we say instead that, if a proposition is evident, and that if one asks oneself whether it is evident, *then* it is evident that the proposition is evident?[20] This is less objectionable, for one cannot ask oneself such a question unless one *does* have the concept of a proposition being evident. In Chapter 3, however, we set forth a simpler principle—what we there called "the *objectivity* principle." The objectivity principle tells us that, if a person knows a given proposition to be true, and if he also *believes* that he knows that proposition to be true, then he *knows that he knows* that proposition to be true.[21]

You may have knowledge, then, without having any *insight* into the epistemic status of what you know. In other words, you may know a proposition h to be true without having any beliefs at all about the fact that h is evident or about what makes h evident for you. You will have *some* degree of insight into your knowledge of h if you have a true belief about what makes h evident for you. You will have a greater degree of insight if, moreover, you have no *false* belief to the effect that some *other* proposition makes h evident for you. And you will have an even greater degree of insight into the status of your knowledge of h, if you also *know* that e makes h evident for you.[22] But our ordinary knowledge about such things as ships, trees, and houses does not require that we have any beliefs about our epistemic situation.

[19]This point is made by Arthur Danto in "On Knowing that we Know," In Avrum Stroll, ed., *Epistemology: New Essays in the Theory of Knowledge* (New York: Harper & Row, 1967), 32–53. But contrast Brentano, who held that the fact that a proposition is evident for a person S is sufficient to give S the concept of a proposition being evident; see *The True and the Evident* (London: Routledge & Kegan Paul, 1966), p. 125.

[20]This principle is suggested by H. A. Prichard: ". . . whenever we know something, we either do, or at least can, by reflecting, directly know that we are knowing." H. A. Prichard, *Knowledge and Perception* (Oxford: The Clarendon Press, 1950), 86.

[21]See Richard Feldman, "Knowing that One Knows," *Philosophical Review*, Vol. XC (1981), pp. 266–282. I am indebted to Feldman for helping me to become clearer about this problem.

[22]See the discussion of "*doxastic warrant*" in Roderick Firth, "Are Epistemic Concepts Reducible to Ethical Concepts?" in A. I. Goldman and J. Kim, eds., *Values and Morals* (Dordrecht: D. Reidel Publishing Company, 1978) pp. 215–230; see p. 218ff. Compare Robert Audi in "The Causal Structure of Indirect Justification," *Journal of Philosophy*, LXXX (1983), pp. 398–495; and John Pollock, *Contemporary Theories of Knowledge*, (Totowa, NJ: Bowman & Littlefield, 1986), p. 81.

INDEX